PRAYER FIRST!
A New Agenda for Catholic Schools

MARY KATHLEEN GLAVICH, SND

PRAYER FIRST!

A New Agenda for Catholic Schools

TWENTY THIRD *23rd*
PUBLICATIONS

*Dedicated to Joan LaChance,
my eighth grade teacher and principal
at St. Francis School, Cleveland, Ohio,
in gratitude for her prayerful support
then and now*

Twenty-Third Publications
A Division of Bayard
One Montauk Avenue, Suite 200
New London, CT 06320
(860) 437-3012 or (800) 321-0411
www.23rdpublications.com

Copyright ©2008 Mary Kathleen Glavich. No part of this publication may be reproduced in any manner without prior written permission of the publisher. Write to the Permissions Editor.

The Scripture passages contained herein are from the *New Revised Standard Version of the Bible*, copyright ©1989, by the Division of Christian Education of the National Council of Churches in the U.S.A. All rights reserved.

ISBN 978-1-58595-703-3
Library of Congress Catalog Card Number: 2008925303
Printed in the U.S.A.

CONTENTS

Introduction	1
1. Why Pray in School?	3
2. Prayer Defined	6
3. Prayer in All Classes	13
4. Prayer in Religion Classes	20
5. Prayer in the School	37
6. Prayer of the Faculty and Staff	49
7. Celebrating the Liturgical Year	54
8. Teaching Traditional Prayers	59
9. Teaching Scripture-Based Prayers	64
10. Teaching Meditation	72
11. Teaching Centering Prayer	76
12. Teaching Mantras	79
Resources for Prayer	83

Appendix 1: Additional Prayers and Activities   89

    1. Jesus Teaches Prayer...................89
    2. The Our Father........................90
    3. A Prayer Lab 94
    4. Examination of Conscience on Prayer 95
    5. Journaling...........................96
    6. Scripture Prayer Service 97
    7. Sample School Prayer...................99
    8. Liturgy Planning Guide.................100
    9. Penitential Prayer Service...............101
    10. The Rosary..........................102
    11. School Retreats......................108
    12. A Holy Triduum Retreat................113
    13. Labyrinth..........................114
    14. Family Prayer Handout................115
    15. Back-to-School Prayer Rally............118
    16. O Antiphons........................120
    17. Stations of the Cross 122
    18. Novena Example 123
    19. Litany Example 123
    20. Scripture Verses......................125
    21. A "Heart Room" Prayer 128
    22. Guided Meditation 129
    23. Introduction to Centering Prayer 131
    24. Treasury of Prayers...................134

Appendix 2: Catholic Prayer Words   147

INTRODUCTION

Many of us first learned to pray at home. Our moms and dads led us in bedtime prayers, showed us how to make the Sign of the Cross, and taught us prayers before meals. Some of us learned to pray the rosary at home, and we learned the Mass prayers by attending liturgy with our families. We learned more complex formulas and forms of prayer in Catholic school or our parish faith formation program. Though school and parish leaders and teachers, including catechists, are called to be leaders of prayer, many feel inadequate. They know it's important to pray and teach about prayer and they realize that parents entrust them with this responsibility, but they aren't sure exactly how to go about it. In fact, certain prayer forms are a mystery to them. Of course, there are many teachers and catechists who feel comfortable teaching prayer but are constantly on the lookout for fresh ideas for forming good prayer habits in young Christians.

In this book, I try to meet these needs in two ways. I offer a "Prayer 101" course by explaining prayer and various prayer forms. In addition, I offer methods and activities for teaching prayer that have worked for others. Based on the assumption that a spirit of prayer ought to permeate an entire Catholic school, I also offer ways for the school community to pray together. Also, because "you can't give what you haven't got," I share ideas for bolstering the prayer life of school leaders and faculty members.

Appendix 1 contains samples of ways to pray with your class—in more detail than in the text of this book. It includes a treasury of prayers, which begins on page 134. At the back of the book in Appendix 2 there is a glossary of prayer words that you will encounter in this book.

Because all prayer ultimately leads to union with God, my prayer for those who use this book echoes St. Paul:

> I bow my knees before the Father....I pray that, according to the riches of his glory, he may grant that you may be strengthened in your inner being with power through his Spirit, and that Christ may dwell in your hearts through faith, as you are being rooted and grounded in love. I pray that you may have the power to comprehend, with all the saints, what is the breadth and length and height and depth, and to know the love of Christ that surpasses knowledge, so that you may be filled with all the fullness of God. (Ephesians 3:14–19)

— 1 —

WHY PRAY IN SCHOOL?

In his book *With Open Hands,* Henri Nouwen vividly describes how necessary prayer is, and I adapt his prayer here:

> The one who never prays…is like the child with asthma; because he is short of breath, the whole world shrivels up before him. He creeps in a corner gasping for air, and is virtually in agony. But the one who prays…is free to boldly stride through the world because he or she can move about without fear.

Prayer is as essential to the spiritual life as breathing is to physical life. Prayer, both personal and communal, is an integral component of our life in Jesus Christ, who not only prayed himself but also taught us how to pray. Clearly Catholic schools and parish faith formation programs must include prayer in the curriculum. But that's not enough. We learn to pray by praying. When students and personnel pray, both alone and together, the atmosphere in the school is then one of prayer, and those who work in the school are giving witness as people of prayer.

A school is not Catholic just because it has religion classes. That would make it little different from the public school down the street. No, the whole school should be saturated with a sense of the sacred, an awareness of Jesus Christ, especially if there is a chapel where he is sacramentally present in the building.

The family is known as the domestic church: a microcosm of the whole church, which is the body of Christ. We might call a Catholic school "the scholastic church," a community of believers eager to share, learn about, and celebrate the gospel message. The vocation of those who work in a Catholic school is no less than the vocation of the apostles, who were called to spread the gospel to all nations. The Catholic school building is as holy as the houses where the early Christians gathered for Eucharist. Educator Thomas Groome suggests that to make ourselves aware of the sacredness of what we're actually about in a Catholic school, some day we should remove our shoes before entering our classroom or office, just as Moses removed his sandals in the presence of God before the burning bush.

In a Catholic school we aren't only teaching science, literature, math, language, and sports, and we aren't only teaching doctrine, the Bible, and church history. Beyond that, we are forming disciples of Jesus, people who know about him and know him, people who live by his values, people prepared to raise families of faith, and people longing to go into the world and work toward the establishment of God's kingdom of justice and peace.

We put youth in touch with Jesus through prayer. Paul's one encounter with Christ changed his life. We hope that by acting as a matchmaker and arranging for our students to meet Jesus in prayer, they too grow to love him more deeply and become more committed to his mission.

If we do not teach our Catholic youth to pray, who will? Sadly, the only time some students pray is in school. Then let's give them good experiences of prayer that whet their appetite for it. Also, it's important to teach them a variety of prayer forms, so that later when their prayer tastes change, they are equipped to pray in a form that better meets their needs.

By showing our students how to pray, we show them a way to make life meaningful and full of promise. We lead them to a Father who loves them when they feel unloved and forgives them when they have failed, to a Savior who teaches them right living and who died for them, and to a Spirit who enlightens them when they are confused. We take them to a friend who gladly shares their joys and who cares when they are distressed. We help them realize that there is someone beyond us who is all-powerful, all-wise, all-just, and all-good, someone who makes sense of the universe. Then our students are more equipped to become good citizens of earth and heaven.

— 2 —

PRAYER DEFINED

A small girl once prayed, "O God, sometimes I think of you even when I'm not praying." Little did she know that when she thought of God, she was praying, according to the traditional definition of prayer: the lifting of the mind and heart to God. Some people prefer St. Teresa of Avila's definition: a conversation with One who you know loves you. In either case, prayer has to do with focusing on God who is always present and active, even when we aren't conscious of him. This awareness and subsequent interaction lead to deeper knowledge and love of the good God.

Prayer has been defined and explained in many different ways. Perhaps one or two of the following speak to you and your students more than others. To develop the "concept" of prayer, invite your students to first discuss some of the definitions given below. Ask them to choose which definition is their favorite and explain why they like it. Then ask them to compose their own definition.

Prayer is wasting time gracefully.

Prayer is putting your hand in God's hand.

Prayer is a hunger.

Prayer is resting in the Lord.

In prayer we let God love us.

Prayer is joy that mounts up to God in thanksgiving.
■ *Isaac the Syrian*

Prayer is our humble answer to the inconceivable surprise of living.   ■ *Rabbi Abraham Heschel*

Prayer is standing before God with the mind in the heart.

Prayer is enjoying the company of a Friend.

Let us leave the surface and, without leaving the world, plunge into God.
■ *Pierre Teilhard de Chardin, S.J.*

Prayer oneth the soul to God.   ■ *Julian of Norwich*

Prayer is love expressed in speech and in silence.
■ *Catherine de Hueck Doherty*

Prayer is a twitch on the line by which God brings us home.   ■ *G.K. Chesterton*

God sits on top of our heart. When we desire to pray, the heart cracks open and God tumbles down inside.   ■ *A Hasidic explanation*

To clasp one's hands in prayer is the beginning of an uprising against the disorder of the world.
■ *Karl Barth*

> Prayer is the mortar that keeps our house together.
> ■ *Blessed Teresa of Calcutta*
>
> Prayer is when heaven and earth kiss each other.
> ■ *Jewish mystic*

Varieties of Prayer

Prayer can be compared to the communication between two people in a love relationship. At first the two talk a lot. They want to learn as much as possible about each other and simultaneously to reveal information, even secrets, to the other. As the relationship deepens over the years, talking is not that necessary. The couple can read each other's minds and communicate with a glance. After much time together, two people in love are even content to be in each other's presence wordlessly.

These same stages hold true for communication in our love relationship with God. We usually begin praying with *vocal (oral) prayer*. This includes formula or so-called traditional prayers such as the Our Father, the Hail Mary, litanies, and additional prayers composed by others. It also can be spontaneous prayer, freely talking aloud to God from our hearts. Then we learn *mental prayer*, for example how to meditate on a Gospel story. The highest form of prayer is *contemplation*, a wordless form of prayer in which we simply enjoy God's presence.

Masters of the spiritual life have guided others in the art of prayer. Their writings and books about them are available. St. Teresa of Avila in particular and St. John of the Cross help everyone to become a mystic, while St. Dominic teaches nine postures of prayer. St. Francis de Sales' classic book *Introduction to the Devout Life* is still relevant, and retreats based on St. Ignatius of Loyola's prayer methods are popular today. More recently, Thomas Merton and Henri Nouwen inspire and teach people to pray.

Purposes for Prayer

Prayer also varies according to purpose. When someone exhibits a good quality or has achieved something remarkable, our response is to acknowledge this with a compliment. Similarly, moved by God's power, goodness, or love, we express *praise and adoration* in our prayer. Sometimes we damage our relationship with God and experience guilt and regret. Seeking forgiveness and reconciliation, we pray prayers of *contrition*. When we are filled with gratitude for gifts, graces, and favors, we respond with prayers of *thanksgiving*. And when we or others are in need of something, we turn trustingly to our good God with prayers of *supplication*. Sometimes we are so taken with God and God's love and mercy that we pray prayers of sheer *love*.

> An acronym to remember the purposes of prayer is ACTS:
> **A**doration,
> **C**ontrition,
> **T**hanksgiving, and
> **S**upplication.
>
> Some prefer to use PACT, which substitutes "Petition" for "Supplication."

The easiest form of prayer is just talking to God about whatever is on our mind. The Carmelite nun Thérèse of Lisieux, known for her "little way," stated, "I have not the courage to search through books for beautiful prayers....Unable either to say them all or choose between them, I do as a child would do who cannot read—I say just what I want to say to God, quite simply, and God never fails to understand." This kind of informal conversation proved to be a very effective form of prayer for Thérèse. She was raised to the status of "saint" not long after her death at the young age of twenty-four.

> **THREE MISCONCEPTIONS ABOUT PRAYER**
>
> *Prayer should take a long time.* No. It's said that short prayers pierce the heavens like arrows. Think of the fast action that results when someone shouts the single word "Fire!"
>
> *Prayer results in a torrent of wonderful thoughts if it is good prayer.* Not so. Sometimes the end product of prayer is merely a sense of peace, a smile, a tear, or a resolution.
>
> *Prayer should be formal.* No again. Forget the thee's and thou's. St. Teresa of Avila advises, "Don't be bashful with such a wonderful Lord."

How God Answers Prayers

What if our prayers aren't "answered"? Does that mean there is no God or that God doesn't love us? Of course not. When God seemingly turns a deaf ear to our request, it could be that God is answering, "No," "Not yet," "I have a better idea," or, as former President Jimmy Carter suggested, "Are you kidding?" The main attitude to adopt is that of Mary and her Son who were both open to God's will no matter what. My favorite story that illustrates the benefit of not always getting what we want is about a small boy who prays for the gift his uncle has—being able to take out his teeth at night and put them in a glass of water. When the boy grew older, he was awfully glad God hadn't answered his prayer.

Often when we pray, our minds flit from one distraction to another. We can try to control this in several ways. Praying at a quiet time in a peaceful place helps. So does focusing on a picture or a candle. Also, writing a prayer demands concentration and therefore eliminates distractions. Sometimes a distraction can be worked into our prayer. Not all distractions are bad. A distraction may be a grace in disguise, for example, if it is the solution to a problem or an idea for an act of charity you can perform.

What Jesus Taught about Prayer

Jesus modeled prayer for us. He prayed alone and with others. As all Jews do, Jesus prayed the psalms, but he also prayed spontaneously. In the gospels we see Jesus praying before major events in his life, such as the choosing of the twelve apostles, the raising of Lazarus, and his passion and death. Sometimes Jesus prayed all night, considered quite a feat by those of us who find one hour a challenge.

Jesus often talked about prayer. He pointed out that we are not to pray in a showy, hypocritical way; but we are to go to our room, close the door, and pray to our Father in secret (Matthew 6:5). On the other hand, Jesus promised that wherever two or three of us are gathered in his name, he is in our midst. He said that we are not to babble but to keep our prayers short and simple (Matthew 6:7). He taught us "to ask and we will receive, seek and we will find, knock and the door will be opened" (Matthew 7:7); and he assured us that whatever we ask for from the Father in his name, we will receive (John 16:23). When the apostles asked him to teach them to pray, Jesus gave them the gift of the Our Father. He told them in the parable of the Pharisee and the tax collector that they were not to boast in prayer, but to be humble (Luke 18:9–14). He also told two parables about perseverance in prayer: the persistent man who needs bread for a visitor (Luke 11:5–8) and the widow pleading with the judge (Luke 18:2–8).

→ See #1 on page 89 for a list of Scripture references related to Jesus and prayer.

→ See #2 on page 90 for a unique way to present the Our Father.

The Best Petition

Jesus also talked about the attitude to have before God when we desire something. During his agony in the garden, Jesus asked the Father that the cup of suffering be taken away from him, but then he prayed, "Not my will but yours be done." Knowing that God is all wise and loving, we trust him to do what is good even if his plan doesn't make sense to us at the time. Like Mary, we leave ourselves totally at God's disposal and confident that whatever God wants is really what is best for us.

Pray Always

Once a sea captain was caught in a terrible storm. He had weathered many a storm before, but this one was unusually fierce. After desperately trying everything to save the ship, as a last resort the sea captain fell to his knees and prayed, "O God, I haven't bothered you for the last twenty years. Save me and I won't bother you for another twenty." Obviously the sea captain did not understand prayer.

St. Paul exhorts us to "pray always." We can heed this advice by being mindful of God throughout the day and remembering that God is ever mindful of us. God is never farther away than the inner recesses of our own hearts. As the mystic Meister Eckhart once said, "God is at home. It is we who have gone out for a walk."

Anyone who is frustrated or discouraged with his or her prayer life can take heart: One thing we can pray for is the grace to pray well! In addition, someone observed that most people are better pray-ers than they think.

— 3 —

PRAYER IN ALL CLASSES

Gone are the days when even math problems in Catholic schools were blatantly religious: Two rosaries, plus three rosaries equals how many? Or when students habitually inscribed A.M.D.G. (All for the greater glory of God) or J.M.J. (Jesus, Mary, Joseph) at the top of each worksheet. Nevertheless, there are other ways that a class, even other than religion class, can reflect that the teachers and students follow Jesus Christ.

Begin with Prayer

Catholic teachers are blessed with an automatic way to begin class: prayer. Use this practice as an opportunity to give your students a taste of prayer in various ways. Here are some ideas.

Together make the Sign of the Cross, the great sign of our salvation and commitment to Jesus. Make it slowly and reverently, and encourage students to offer themselves to God.

Pray one of the traditional prayers such as the Our Father, Hail Mary, Apostles' Creed, Glory Be to the Father, or Act of Contrition. With repetition these basic prayers are more likely to become part of the students' personal prayer repertoire.

Call for a few moments of silent prayer. You might direct the students to become aware of their breathing or heartbeat and then recall that God is present.

Display a prayer and pray it all week. This can be a short prayer, such as "Jesus, for you I live. Jesus, for you I die. Jesus, I am yours in life and in death" or a longer prayer such as the Memorare.

Design a Prayer Pocket and invite the students to put their favorite prayers or original prayers in it. Each day draw one prayer out to pray.

Have the students submit prayers for a booklet to use for class. Type the prayers on sheets of paper and duplicate them so that when they are folded in fourths, they form a booklet. Give everyone a personal copy.

Plan to have a different student for each class prepare a prayer and lead it. The students can sign up on a chart or take turns according to seating order.

Compose a prayer yourself and link it with life by incorporating world events or current school events. Theologian Karl Barth recommended, "Read with the newspaper in one hand and the Bible in the other."

Read a few Scripture verses, perhaps a reading from the day's Mass, and respond with a short prayer. (The Web site www.dailygospel.org will email you the readings and a commentary every day.)

Pray a few verses from the psalms, the Bible's prayerbook.

Sing a known hymn, perhaps accompanied by an instrument, a tape, or a CD.

Use a book of prayers compiled especially for children or teenagers. (See the resource section at the back of this book.)

→ See #24 on page 134 for a collection of prayers.

Make an Intention

Catholics believe in the Communion of Saints, which means that all saints in heaven, all souls in purgatory, and "all sorts" on earth are bound together in the Body of Christ. Because we are all united in Christ, the good performed by one or several members can be applied to others. We can "offer up" facets of our lives, especially our sufferings, for different intentions. You and your students can make intentions for your hard work done in class in these ways:

- State an intention based on a current need.
- Ask the students for intentions. You might want to limit these to one or two.
- Pray for the two intentions that the Holy Father proposes to the Church each month—a general one and one for the missions. These can be located at www.apostleshipofprayer.org.
- Offer each class for one of the students. Periodically pass around a calendar and have your students sign up for the day(s) they would like to be prayed for. They will probably sign up for significant days like their birthdays.

Spiritual Bouquets

A longstanding Catholic practice has been giving a "spiritual bouquet" as a gift to someone. The students promise to offer specific prayers and good deeds for that person and his or her intentions and state this in a card. For example, for a class of twenty students these promises can be put in this form: "We each offer three Hail Marys, three Our Fathers, and three acts of charity." Or the prayers can be added together and listed as "sixty Hail Marys, sixty Our Fathers, and sixty acts of charity." These "gifts" can be creative, such as "five extra minutes of prayer each day for a week," "donating half of my weekly allowance to the missions," or "attending a Saturday morning Mass."

Christian Ambience

Make the décor of your classroom proclaim that your school is a community of faith. The following are possibilities that also serve as reminders to pray:

- A prayer table with a Bible and devotional objects. Cover the table with an attractive cloth or a scarf and set flowers and a candle on it. Change the table to reflect the seasons of the church year, feast days, and saints' days. Invite the students to bring religious items from home for the table.
- A crucifix
- Statues or pictures of Jesus, Mary, and other saints
- A bulletin board devoted to a religious theme
- Religious posters
- Palm behind the crucifix or other religious image. You or a student might weave the palm in one of the traditional designs. Directions for these can be found at www.italiansrus.com/palms/palmpatterns.htm.

During Class

Opportunities for practicing the faith often occur during a lesson. When someone sneezes during class, it only takes a few seconds to say, "God bless you" (not just "Bless you.") When sirens sound, pray a brief prayer for anyone in danger: "God, protect those in trouble and their helpers." Likewise, if a major world or local event occurs during class time, pray together about it. Last but not least, when a student is named for the saint of the day, greet him or her with, "Happy nameday!" and say a brief prayer to the saint asking for blessings on the student.

When there is a lull in the class, for instance when the students are waiting for a speaker to arrive or a television program to come on, suggest that they use the time for short prayers. Similarly when the students are waiting for a turn or standing in line or finish their work early, mention that they might pray.

Spiritualizing Your Lessons

Textbooks for secular subjects in Catholic schools usually don't include information pertaining to our faith. A little creativity in spiritualizing the learning experience and in incorporating Catholic facts can go a long way in helping your students know and appreciate their faith. Here are some examples.

- In science class, after reading about or viewing an astonishing aspect of our universe and our planet Earth, remark how wise and good God is to design such marvels. You might respond with a prayer such as, "Great are the works of the Lord, studied by all who delight in them!" (Psalm 111:2).

- In health class, there is reason to echo the sentiments of this verse: "I praise you, for I am fearfully and wonderfully made" (Psalm 139:14).

- In English class, include some Catholic literature in your lesson plan. For example, a poetry lesson might include Francis Thompson's "The Hound of Heaven" or poems of Gerard Manley Hopkins, SJ.
- In history class, insert some information about prayer, such as the origin of Gregorian chant and the role of the miracle and mystery plays in the Middle Ages. Relay interesting tidbits, for example:
  - Charlemagne loved the psalms; his nickname was David.
  - When the founding fathers of the United States couldn't agree on the Constitution, Benjamin Franklin quoted, "Unless the Lord, build the house, they labor in vain who build it" (Psalm 127:1) and suggested that they begin the next day with prayer. As a result, to this day Congress opens with prayer.
  - Abraham Lincoln once said, "I have been driven many times to my knees by the overwhelming conviction that I had nowhere else to go. My wisdom and that of all round me seemed insufficient for the day."
  - The flag of the European Union has twelve stars designed by the artist to honor Mary as she is depicted in the Book of Revelation.
- In art class, study religious art, including icons, which are painted as the artist fasts and prays.
- In music class, include religious music, past and modern. And in studying the lives of composers share items like the fact that when Haydn had trouble composing, he prayed the rosary.

- Use physical education classes as an arena for teaching Christian virtues and qualities, such as kindness, justice, fortitude, and forgiveness. Have your students pray for these qualities even more than they pray to win a game.
- Math affords the chance to point out the ingenuity of the Creator-God, who is as mysterious and infinite as numbers. Be on the lookout for related items such as this quotation and share them with your students: "God is a circle whose center is everywhere and whose circumference is nowhere" (Hermes Trismegistus, an ancient alchemist).

Infusing secular lessons with a spirit of faith and prayer requires time and effort. Once you make up your mind to do this, however, you may find that the ideas will flow.

— 4 —

PRAYER IN RELIGION CLASS

Of course, the main arena where prayer is taught and practiced is the religion class. Religion teachers can implement the suggestions offered in the previous chapter as well as the ones provided here that are specifically for religion lessons.

The first rule for teaching religion is *teach religion*. That may sound obvious, but what happens sometimes is that teachers transform a religion course into a course in psychology, guidance, or social science. Or, due to a lack of confidence in teaching the faith, when time is short, it's religion class that is cut. Or sometimes instead of teaching religion using educational principles and methods, catechists spend the time letting the students discuss a topic (which can be merely shared ignorance) or do service projects. These activities are good in themselves and may entertain the students and keep them happy, but they do the students (and their parents) an injustice by depriving them of the tools needed for a solid life in Christ—like knowing ways to pray.

Most basal religion textbook series contain a strand or at least a lesson or two on prayer, and many weave prayer activities throughout the lessons. Do not skip these, mistakenly thinking that it's more important to cover the other material. Prayers and celebrations give students an opportunity to interact directly with God, experience community, and let the mysteries they learn sink into their hearts. In addition to your series' lessons, you can adapt some of the following ideas.

A Prayer Corner

Designate a certain part of the room as a prayer corner and decorate it accordingly, for example with a Bible, a crucifix, and maybe a rocking chair. You might provide prayer rugs, mats, or pillows for the students to sit on during prayer times. Have the students gather in the prayer corner for prayer when it is part of your lesson. Also, encourage them to go there for individual prayer when their work is finished.

Prayers for One Another

Put all of the students' names and yours as well into a box. Pass around the box, having each person draw a name for someone to pray for in a special way during the month or for a week at a time.

Intentions

Choose a way to allow the students to express intentions. Here are three options:

- Allocate part of a blackboard or bulletin board as the Prayer Corner on which students post special needs that require prayer.

- Provide a prayer basket in which students place prayer requests. These may be read at the beginning of class, or the basket may be passed around and students may draw out a request to pray for during the week.
- Give the students narrow slips of paper on which to write intentions. Have them staple or glue these together as links on a prayer chain. Display the chain in the room and keep supplies available for adding to the chain.

Use Comic Strips

For a development lesson on prayer that guarantees you'll have students' rapt attention, collect comic strips that deal with prayer. You'll be surprised how many you'll find. You may want to mount and laminate the comic strips. Label each one with a letter of the alphabet and write this letter in your lesson plan when the comic strip matches a concept. Before the lesson, distribute the comic strips to students. Then as you proceed through the plan, call out each letter when you come to it and have the student holding the matching comic strip read it to the class.

Prayer Packets

For a class on prayer or a retreat prepare (or have the students prepare) prayer experiences using prayer packets. Use folders or large envelopes and assemble materials on different themes: pictures, prayers, cassette tapes or CDs, and other things that could be used for at least three prayer activities. Include instructions. Have the students choose a packet and follow the instructions.

A Prayer Lab

Organize prayer activities at stations around the room. The activities should all take approximately the same amount of time. Form the students into groups and have them move from one station to another and carry out the activities at each. Make sure there are complete instructions at each station.

→ See #3 on page 94 for a sample prayer lab.

Tap Models of Prayer

Faith is caught more than taught. As you teach about prayer, let other people be teacher aides in these ways:

- Invite a speaker to talk about prayer and its role in his or her life.
- Form a panel of guests who vary in age and occupation and have them tell about their prayer experiences and then entertain questions from the students.
- As an assignment, have the students ask five people to tell their favorite way to pray. Let the students report on these to the class.
- Have the students learn from their peers by having them share prayer experiences.
- Give examples of saints or well-known people and the times and ways they have prayed. Models abound:
    - St. Monica prayed for years for her son Augustine, who was finally converted, became a bishop, and ultimately a saint.
    - American Indians referred to St. Rose Philippine Duchesne as "the woman who prays."
    - In his letters, St. Paul prayed for all the churches.

- St. Thomas More, chancellor of England, prayed every morning from two to six o'clock.
- Pope John XXIII prayed the rosary every day.

Be Current

Bring to class newspaper or magazine clippings illustrating how and why people have prayed. Better still, have the students bring in the examples and share them. Post the items.

WEBSITES LINKED TO PRAYER

Introduce the students to websites that foster prayer:

The Divine Office	liturgyhours.org
The Sunday readings and short reflection	catholicnews.com/word2lif.htm
Prayers by saints	catholicdoors.com
Sacred Space	jesuit.ie/prayer
The Psalms	praythepsalms.com *and* thedailypsalm.com
The rosary	theholyrosary.org
Stations of the Cross	www.catholic.org
The labyrinth	thepace-project.org/fingerlab.html *and* yfc.co.uk/labyrinth/online.html
2,774 prayers	catholicdoors.com/prayers

DEVELOPING THE HABIT OF PRAYER

A college student once told me that he considers any day that doesn't begin with prayer a wasted day. How do you lead students to form the habit of daily prayer? Here are some suggestions.

Assessing Prayer Life

As the first step in getting your students to make prayer a habit, engage them in an activity that helps them evaluate their current prayer life. Here are suggestions for the students:

- Keep a chart of daily activities for a week and see how much time you spend grooming, working, being educated, reading, playing games, talking, sleeping, eating, and praying.
- Answer prayer-related questions either privately or in a group: When do you pray? Why? How long do you pray? What do you pray about? What is your favorite prayer? What prevents you from praying?
- Write three things you really want, three wonderful things you are grateful for, and three things you are worried about. Then check the things you remembered to pray about. What do the number of checks reveal about your prayer life?
- Each night fill out a daily examination of conscience leaflet with boxes to be checked for morning prayers, meal prayers, evening prayers, extra prayers, and Bible reading.

→ See #4 on page 95 for questions that could be used for an examination of conscience on prayer.

Carving Time for Prayer

Teach the importance of making time for prayer. Tell the students that American author Flannery O'Connor described waiting for inspiration in a way that also describes waiting for the Lord to speak: "Every morning between 9 and 12, I go to my room and sit before a piece of paper. Many times I just sit for three hours with no ideas coming to me. But I know one thing: If an idea does come between 9 and 12, I am there ready for it."

Encourage the students to a set a specific time for their prayer, such as early in the morning or right before they go to bed.

Finding a Place

Suggest that the students find a special place where they can talk to God in peace and quiet without distractions. This can be their room, an attic space, the basement, a closet, the library, or outside.

Being Silent

Teach the students the value of silence for hearing God's voice. You might tell them the story of the prophet Elijah to whom God spoke not in an earthquake or strong wind or fire but in a tiny whisper (1 Kings 19:9–13). Discuss good things that happen in silence, why we need silence, and where we keep silence and why. Use settling activities to bring young children to silence: Have them repeat, "I'm as snug as a bug in a rug" over and over and invite them to have "listening" hands and "listening" feet.

Being Relaxed

Invite the students to focus on their breathing. Tell them to inhale slowly, count to five, and then exhale slowly. Repeat this three times. Teach the students to relax their muscles before prayer. Have them begin with the top of their head, tightening the muscles there for a few seconds and then loosening them. Then have them focus in turn on their forehead, eyes, mouth, cheeks, neck, shoulders, arms, hands, chest, thighs, lower legs, and feet, each time tightening and then loosening the muscles. Or have the students imagine that they are floating on a cloud or on a river.

Prayer Postures

Suggest that the students experiment with different postures for prayer: standing, sitting, kneeling, bowing, lying flat on their backs, prostrating, sitting cross-legged, walking, holding arms outstretched, resting hands palms up and opened on the lap, or holding hands with others. They might try the Lotus pose: sit with the legs crossed so that the feet rest at the bend of the knees and then rest hands on heels with forefingers and thumbs touching to form a circle.

Filling Time

Propose to the students that they use odd moments to pray. Give the following examples of down time when they could pray and ask them to suggest other times as well.

- While on hold on the phone
- While waiting for a red light to change

- While standing in a checkout line
- While waiting for a bus
- While waiting for something to download

Feelings

To motivate the students to pray at times they don't feel like it, share this passage from Julian of Norwich's *Revelation*:

> Our Lord is greatly cheered by our prayer. He looks for it, and he wants it....So he says, "Pray inwardly, even if you do not enjoy it. It does you good, though you feel nothing, see nothing, yes even though you think you are dry, empty, sick or weak. At such a time your prayer is most pleasing to me."

Sleeping

Tell the students that it's all right if they fall asleep while praying. St. Thérèse of Lisieux explained that she did not regret sleeping during prayer. She pointed out that little children please their parents just as much when they sleep as when they are awake. The heavenly Father loves us as we sleep.

Remembering to Pray

Suggest that in the evening the students place their shoes under the bed so that the next morning when they kneel to get their shoes, they remember to pray. An alternate reminder is to tie a sock around the bedpost. A "prayer stone" kept on the pillow and moved to the floor at night serves the same purpose.

Examen of Conscience

A good practice for being more mindful of God and God's action in one's life is the nightly examen of conscience. Teach your students these steps: Recall God's presence. Think of things during the day that you are grateful for. Then replay the day, looking for times when you accepted God's guidance and times when you didn't cooperate with it. Ask forgiveness for your failings. Then ask for help to respond better the next day.

Praying in Class

Prepare the students for prayer. Eliminate distractions by pulling down the shades if necessary. You might play soothing music. Remind the students that they are in the presence of God or recall that Jesus promised that wherever two or three are gathered in his name, he is with them (Matthew 18:20). Do relaxation exercises with the students as described in the previous section "Being Relaxed." Depending on the type of prayer, the students might close their eyes and put their heads down if they wish. Stand in back of the room so that the students feel more comfortable knowing that you're not watching their faces.

A Personal Prayerbook

Encourage the students to compile their own personal prayer books. They could include favorite prayers of the saints, prayers they come across and like, as well as their own original prayers. They might decorate the pages with religious art and symbols.

Traveling Statues

Arrange for an icon or a statue of Jesus, Mary, or a saint, or a saint's relic to travel from home to home accompanied by prayers to be prayed by the student or, better, by the whole family. This can be done to honor God or the saint or to pray for a certain intention. For example, some schools have a traveling wooden cross with prayers to pray for vocations.

Writing Prayers

It is said that we don't really know what we think until we write it. Have the students write their own prayers. They might use popular prayers, saints' prayers, or the psalms as a model. These prayers can be collected, copied, and shared with others in the form of a booklet. They might also be posted on a website. One powerful prayer is to compose a letter to Jesus. Begin "Dear Jesus," and end "Love, *(Name)*." Then they can write another letter beginning "Dear *(Name)*" and ending "Love, Jesus." For this second letter, tell them to just let the thoughts flow. Don't force them or try to imagine what Jesus would be saying to them.

Journaling

Introduce your students to keeping a journal of thoughts and prayers. Provide or have the students purchase spiral notebooks and have them spend a few minutes at the end of class recording their reflections. Or make journaling a home assignment and give the students specific questions or open-ended statements to guide their writing. To allow them to write freely, you might have them clip together or cover sections they don't want you to see. Promise not to read those sections and then keep your promise.

→ See #5 on page 96 for ways to jump-start journaling.

Reflections

A number of popular reflections exist, such as "One Solitary Life," "Parable of the Two Seas," "Desiderata," "Footprints," "Letter from a Friend," and "Persons Are Gifts." You probably receive them periodically in your e-mail from friends and acquaintances. Weave these reflections into your lesson as food for thought, or use them as springboards for prayer.

Prayer Services

For special occasions or as a culminating activity for a lesson, hold a prayer service centered around a theme. Involve your students in the planning. Include Scripture, reflection time, at least one hymn, and, if possible, a ritual such as a procession.

→ See #6 on page 97 for a prayer service on Scripture called "The Gift of God's Word."

Spontaneous Prayer

Many Catholics become tongue-tied when it comes to spontaneous prayer. The best way to teach it is to let the students hear you pray this way. Find occasions to do so.

Never put students on the spot by asking them to pray spontaneously. Instead, invite them by saying, "Does anyone wish to?" You can elicit prayer from children with ease by gluing pictures on a cardboard box and passing it around. Ask each child to say, "I thank you, God, for…" and name something in one of the pictures. It helps to have students jot down ideas ahead of time for "spontaneous" prayer.

Processions

Hold processions as part of prayer services. Explain that prayerfully moving from one place to another is a form of worship. The students can make banners to carry in their processions, or they can carry other things. For young children you might call the processions "parades."

Prayer Walks

Take your class on a prayer walk. Encourage the students to be aware of God on the way. Invite them to be sensitive to what they see and hear and to consider what God is saying to them through it. If the walk is done at school, at different stops have the students pray prayers related to those places: where they wait for rides home, a prayer for safety; in the cafeteria, a prayer for those who are hungry; at the principal's office, a prayer for him or her; in the playground, a prayer for good friendships; at the faculty room, a prayer for the teachers; and so forth.

Go to Jesus

If there is a chapel or church on the grounds, take your students there for prayer or for a particular lesson. This is an opportunity to teach church etiquette: being silent, genuflecting or bowing, taking holy water. If the Blessed Sacrament is present, allow the students quiet time for a heart-to-heart talk with Our Lord.

Be Creative

One day in May I had my class make a pilgrimage to statues of Mary inside the school and on the school property as well as at the adjacent Catholic college. We prayed a decade of the rosary at each site. Consider possibilities for prayer that your grounds hold. Use your ingenuity in planning unique prayer experiences.

Use Props

To make a space more conducive to prayer, play soft instrumental music in the background. You might also light a candle (if fire laws permit), burn incense (if no one is allergic to it), or dim the lights. It also helps to display an inspiring poster or have the students look at individual pictures held in their hands or placed on their desks.

Art Prayer

Involve the students in prayer through art in the following ways:

- Have them draw a picture of their favorite place and set it in front of them as they pray.
- Direct them to draw what they want to pray about and then have them take turns expressing their prayers. They can place their drawings in the prayer corner after they pray.
- Give the students a square of aluminum foil and have them form it into a symbol of their favorite gospel story while they speak to Jesus about that story. Afterwards, they can get into groups and share their symbols, explaining why they chose the stories and what the symbols represent. Instead of foil, you might use pipe cleaners, clay, or paper, which the students can tear into shapes.
- Have the students print prayers or inspiring sayings on buttons, badges, plaques, T-shirts, cups, bumper stickers, doorknob hangers, bookmarks, paperweights, seashells, rocks, or pennants.

Blessings

Priests aren't the only ones who can give blessings. Anyone can. You might bless each student as part of a prayer service or at the end of class. This is done by simply saying, "May God bless you." These or similar words can be accompanied by actions: raising your hand or hands over the students, placing a sign of the cross on their foreheads or palms perhaps using holy oil, sprinkling them with holy water, and, depending on the age and attitude of your students, even by laying your hands on their heads. You can also invite the students to bless one another.

Prayerful Greetings

On your students' birthdays, namedays, or other special occasions, present them with religious notecards that have a personal message and prayer from you inside.

Use Media

Read selections from books and articles and show movies that tell about prayer or evoke prayer.

Reaching into the Home

Think of prayer-related homework and projects that involve the whole family. One school held a contest to see which family could design the most unique rosary. Invite families to special prayer activities, such as a dramatized stations of the cross or a May crowning.

UNIQUE PRAYER ACTIVITIES

Alphabet Prayer
Challenge students to pray a prayer of thanks for things that each begin with a letter of the alphabet, and try to go from A to Z.

Doodle Prayer
Direct the students to doodle on a piece of paper and then pray about what they see in their doodle.

Title Prayer
Ask the students to choose a title for God or for Jesus and then write a prayer related to that title.

Meditation Kit
This idea helps develop the habit of prayer. It was suggested by Patricia Brisson in an issue of *Religion Teacher's Journal*. Each week a different student takes the kit home. The kit is a large pencil case that holds a crucifix, a small spiral notepad, and a three-minute egg timer. In the front of the notebook are these directions:

1. Find a spot where you will not be disturbed and sit in a comfortable position.
2. Choose a phrase on which to meditate. For example:
    Thank you, Lord.
    Forgive me, Lord.
    I praise you, Jesus.
    I love you, Jesus.
    What should I do, Jesus?

3. Write today's date and your meditation choice in the notebook.
4. Hold the crucifix in your hand or place it before you.
5. Recall that God is present.
6. Turn over the timer and begin to meditate.
7. At the end of the week write one or two sentences telling what you thought about the meditations. Was three minutes long enough? Did you feel as though you were really praying? Do you think the kit helped you? Would you like to do it again? Was it boring or too long? Please be honest.

— 5 —

PRAYER IN THE SCHOOL

School-wide prayer activities reinforce the prayer that happens in classrooms and homes. At times you might invite the students' families as well as the Christian community at large to prayer events. Here are some ideas for making your school a holy, wholly Catholic institution.

Eucharist

Celebrate the Eucharist together as a school or as grade levels. This, the most perfect prayer, nourishes and builds the Christian community as nothing else does. Involve the students and school personnel as much as possible in planning and celebrating these liturgies. Prepare the students by discussing the feast and the readings either in religion class or by means of an introduction to the Mass.

→ See #8 on page 100 for a liturgy planning guide.

School Patron

Somewhere in a prominent place in the school or on the grounds there probably is an attractive image of the school patron. In one school named Regina High School, for Our Lady as queen, a wall in its main hall is covered with Marian art including multicultural images. Similarly, the administration wing of Notre Dame College of Ohio has a special Marian room in which many statues of Mary from all over the world are displayed.

Celebrate your school patron and his or her feast day each year by a Mass or at least a prayer service and some special activity for the student body.

A School Prayer

Does your school have its own prayer? If not, arrange to have one written by one of these methods:

- hold a contest among the students or families
- get input from the students and then have the oldest students use these ideas to formulate a prayer
- ask a group of students who are gifted writers to compose a prayer together.

Some talented person in the school community might even set your prayer to music.

→ See #7 on page 99 for a sample school prayer.

Yearly Motto

Choosing a religious motto for the school year gives direction to the year and keeps everyone mindful that a Catholic school is a school with a difference. The motto could originate with the students themselves. Display the motto in a main hall, print it on leaflets and letters, and carry out activities linked to it.

PA Prayer

Set the school day in a prayerful context by opening with morning prayer and closing with prayer said by all. See the resource section at the back of this book for helpful prayer resources. The students can take turns leading these prayers and even writing them. You might devote a year to a specific type of prayer and use it to begin each day, for example, the psalms, prayers by the saints, or prayers from Scripture.

→ See #23 on page 134 for a collection of prayers.

School Prayer Book

Assign students or families a day or a topic and ask them to write an appropriate prayer. Compile the prayers into a book. These could be duplicated and distributed to all the families.

St. Thomas Aquinas

The patron of Catholic schools is St. Thomas Aquinas, whose feastday is January 28. Celebrate this day with prayers to St. Thomas and perhaps a school Mass. Throughout the school year pray to St. Thomas for school needs and keep the students and their families aware of his role in interceding for your school.

A Prayer Room

Designate one room as a prayer room where individuals and

classes can go to pray. Decorate and furnish the room so that the effect is simplicity and beauty. Display religious art and supply the room with prayer aids such as rosaries and prayer books. You might place several large pillows there to sit on while praying.

Grace before Meals

If possible, lead the students in praying grace before meals. Remember to pray this prayer at school meetings and other special events that include meals.

Reconciliation

Offer the students opportunities to celebrate the sacrament of reconciliation. The season of Lent and school retreats are especially appropriate times for conversion of heart. Prepare the students well for the sacrament, for example, hold an examination of conscience in common and review the Rite of Penance. The sacrament might take place in the context of a penitential prayer service.

→ See #9 on page 101 for a penitential prayer service.

TRADITIONAL PRAYER EVENTS

Organizing a Living Rosary

A "Living Rosary" is formed by students themselves (and maybe teachers). Each person represents a bead and holds flowers or vigil lights. When it is time for their respective prayer, students come to the microphone, lead the prayer, and then place their item before an image of the Virgin Mary. The Glory Be to the Father prayer may be said by the student who prays the last Hail Mary in each decade. The students praying the Our Fathers announce each mystery. Marian songs may be sung to enhance the devotion. The mysteries can be presented in creative ways.

→ See #10 on pages 102-107 for information on the rosary and for some activities for the Luminous Mysteries.

A May Crowning

The Church has an official rite for the crowning of Mary that you can adapt for your school. Decide how to choose the person who will crown Mary. You might wish to have representatives of different grade levels act as attendants and process to the statue with the "crowners." They can carry flowers and place these in a vase near the statue. Perhaps you can invite the school's first communicants to lead the procession.

→ See page 143 for the Litany of the Blessed Virgin Mary that could be part of the May crowning.

Stations of the Cross

These can be prayed in the traditional way in a church or chapel. You might want to try a more creative approach by incorporating music and dance, which would have more impact on the students. The students could also

- present each station through a homemade prayers or poems,
- pose behind a sheet with light shining directly on them to create a silhouette representing someone from each station, or

- prepare a modern multimedia presentation that incorporates some words or events from each station.

→ See #17 on page 122 for information about the Stations of the Cross.

Grade-Level Retreats

Arrange for a "retreat" for each grade level, a prayerful time for students to renew their relationship with God. To make it special, hold it somewhere off campus. Involve parents in planning and carrying out the retreat. One school chooses a retreat theme, and each grade level's retreat is related to that theme. During the retreat, the students make something that is added to a progressive bulletin board or wall in the school.

Usual components of retreats are talks by speakers, time for private prayer, communal prayer, a stimulating video, the celebration of the Eucharist, and an opportunity for celebrating the sacrament of reconciliation. Inspirational reading material should be available for the retreatants.

→ See #11 on page 108 for a sample retreat program.

Special Day Retreats

Before special events in the students' lives, celebrate a day of prayer. For example, before First Holy Communion conduct a Jesus Day, before Confirmation have a Spirit Day, and before graduation celebrate a Moving-On Day. You can also prepare for these occasions by praying "novenas" (nine days of prayer) or triduums (three days of prayer). Involve children in deciding what these prayers will be and then provide families with the suggested prayers so they can participate.

Be sure to also plan prayer activities to celebrate the Holy Triduum, the three most solemn days in the church year.

→ See #12 on page 113 for suggested prayer activities to celebrate the Triduum.

The School Chapel

Schools with chapels will want to make them user-friendly for students. Keep a supply of prayer books, rosaries, and station booklets available for their use. Encourage students to leave these items in the chapel for others to use. You might also have a book at the doorway where students and school personnel can record prayer intentions.

Family Intentions

Invite families to share their special intentions with the school via a phone call, a letter, or e-mail. Publicize these intentions in family newsletters and post them on your school website. Also, incorporate them into school prayer and Masses. An Intention Book might be kept near the school office where students could record their family intentions. For a special intention, you might keep a vigil light burning as a sign of your prayers rising to heaven.

Parallel to the intentions also publicize "Reasons to Be Thankful" when prayers are answered.

In Memoriam

Display a book or plaque with the names of deceased students and their family members. Periodically arrange for a Memorial Mass or a prayer service for them.

Exposition and Benediction

If you are fortunate to have a chapel or church nearby, plan to have the students experience exposition of the Blessed Sacrament and Benediction. This is a traditional form of prayer in the church during which the priest places a consecrated host in a sun-shaped container called a monstrance. This is placed on the altar for a period of time during which people come to pray. At the end of this prayer time, the priest blesses all present with the monstrance. This is called Benediction.

Blessings

Arrange for special blessings, such as the blessing of throats on the feast of St. Blaise, the blessings of animals on the feast of St. Francis of Assisi, the blessing of Bibles and rosaries, and the blessing of a new shrine or statue for the school. These blessings offer students new experiences and reinforce the teaching that God loves them and blesses them.

Prayer Groups

Establish a prayer group as an extracurricular activity. The group might meet before or after school once a week for prayer together. The group could create a name and choose a patron saint. Encourage students in these groups to try a variety of ways to pray: using the Bible, writing petitions, silent prayer, the rosary, the stations of the cross, prayers of thanksgiving, and sharing their own written prayer.

Prayer Leaders

Initiate a special ministry at the school for overseeing and carrying out prayer activities. The student prayer leaders can help plan Masses, retreats, and other prayer activities. Some older students might serve as prayer mentors, meeting with younger students one-on-one for prayer.

Bible Study

Begin a Bible study program for the students. There are programs available that are specially geared towards teenagers, such as one published by the Little Rock Scripture Study. Bible Study can be carried out as part of the regular class or as an extracurricular activity. In my parish, teens meet at 6:30 AM on Wednesday mornings, discuss the Scripture reading together, and then go out for breakfast before they go to school. St. Mary's Press offers a training program for student and adult leaders of Bible study groups.

Prayer Theme

Choose a certain form of prayer to focus on all year: the Eucharist, centering prayer, psalms, the Divine Office, Scripture-based prayer, or mantras. The school as a whole could be introduced to this form of prayer and then you might emphasize it in class.

Time Out for Prayer

Some schools have a sustained reading time when everyone reads for a designated time every day. You might schedule a "time out for prayer" each day when everyone prays at a designated time.

Pilgrimages

Arrange pilgrimages for your different grade levels. They could visit a Marian shrine in the area, the diocesan cathedral, or a particular church with historical relevance. Invite parents to come as chaperones.

A Prayer Labyrinth

If there is an institution nearby that has a canvas labyrinth, borrow it for a time and teach the students to walk the labyrinth. An alternative is a labyrinth that is on a sheet of paper and "walked" with the finger. This prayer began as a substitute for a pilgrimage to Jerusalem in the Middle Ages. Several European cathedrals had labyrinths in their floors. The only remaining of these is in the cathedral in Chartres. People pray as they walk along the labyrinth path to its center, which represents God, and then they retrace their steps going back out to the world.

→ See #13 on page 114 for a labyrinth that can be enlarged and copied.

WAYS TO REINFORCE PRAYER HABITS

Prayer Partners

Older and younger students can be paired as prayer partners. Or classes or individual students can be paired with an alum, a parishioner, or a senior citizen living in an assisted living residence or a nursing home. Actual times together for prayer can be planned, or the partners can simply promise to keep each other in their prayers. Arrange for the partners to exchange photos of themselves.

Prayer Festival

Have the school participate in a mini prayer festival that could be planned by a committee or by one grade level. Prayer activities can be carried out at different stations. As groups complete a prayer or activity, they move to the next station. Try to include at least five stations for a variety of prayer experiences.

Prayer Panel

For one of your school assemblies invite people from different walks of life to witness to their faith by sharing the ways they pray. Allow time for questions.

Prayer Pep Rally

Organize a prayer pep rally for which students from different grade levels perform and lead cheers to celebrate and honor God. Prayer topics to cheer about include Jesus, the Holy Spirit, Mary, the saints, the church, the virtues, and the gift of life itself.

Family Prayer

At parent meetings focus on family prayer. Include time for parents to share ways their family prays together. Distribute and discuss a handout with suggestions for fostering family prayer.

→ See #14 on page 115 for ideas for a family handout.

Prayer Support Group

Begin a prayer group of parents, grandparents, and alumni that meets in the school weekly or monthly to pray for school intentions. For example, at one school after a child was attacked while waiting for a bus, moms began to gather at the school to pray the rosary together for the safety of their children.

Prayer Calendar
Each month send a calendar page home with a short prayer or a school-centered intention typed in each block.

A Back-to-School Prayer Rally
Invite parents to join the students in an evening of prayer for blessings on the school year, the faculty, staff, students, and their families.

→ See #15 on page 118 for a sample back-to-school prayer rally.

Awards and Gifts
Give prayer-related school awards and gifts: a Bible, a rosary, a finger rosary, a metal or cloth labyrinth, a religious medal, a religious picture, or prayer books for children or youth.

National Day of Prayer
President Reagan permanently established the first Thursday in May as the National Day of Prayer. Plan some school-wide prayer activity for this day, such as a prayer rally or special prayers at the beginning and end of the school day.

— 6 —

PRAYER OF THE FACULTY AND STAFF

We ourselves must be people of prayer. Only then will we be convincing models of Christian discipleship for those we teach. Pope Paul VI wrote, "Modern men and women listen more willingly to witnesses than to teachers, and if they listen to teachers, it is because they are also witnesses" (*Evangelii Nuntiandi*).

A fundamental way to be a person of prayer is to have a contemplative stance toward life. For one thing this means to be sensitive to the beauties of our earthly home and allow ourselves time to wonder at God's wisdom and goodness that provided them. It means to look intensely at things—a sunset, a bird, a loved one, your own face—and ponder the deeper realities they point to. It also means being open to God: viewing life's happenings aware that God's providence is guiding all and listening for God's direction. Nurturing these God-centered attitudes gives us a peaceful, prayerful aura, transforming us into reliable models for our students.

Preface Activities with Prayer
School personnel could make a habit of beginning school functions with prayer. Here are some opportunities:
- a meeting of the faculty, a committee, or a school organization
- a parent conference
- a school assembly
- school-wide exams
- a game

Teachers might pray before these activities:
- preparing a lesson
- a class observation
- a parent conference
- open house
- making out grades
- meeting with a student
- calling a student's parents

Prayer for Students
An esteemed educator in my community once said that we should talk to God about our students more than we talk to our students about God. Make a practice of keeping the names of your students in your prayer book or Bible and praying for them as a group as well as individually.

Sometimes in the case of a particularly challenging student, when all else fails, prayer works, privately or in the presence of the student. In one case, a principal was at her wit's end dealing with an unruly, belligerent fourth grader. Finally she called the lad to her office and said, "I don't know how to make you a good boy. I'm going to have to ask Jesus for help." Then she prayed out loud to Jesus for the boy. This so impressed the troublemaker that it brought about a change in his behavior.

Don't forget to make blessings on your whole school one of your prayer intentions too.

Revealing Your Own Prayer Life

Let your students know that you pray. At first you might feel uncomfortable doing this. For some reason, we're usually as private in talking about our prayer as we are about sex. That's unfortunate because as authority figures in our students' lives we have power by our example to influence the value they place on prayer, whether they pray, and how they pray.

While teaching about prayer or in taking advantage of one of those teachable moments in life, share with the students your prayer stories, how you pray, how your prayers were answered, what you have learned about prayer, and what your favorite prayer or favorite way of praying is. I like to tell my students that my most frequent prayer is "Help!"

Witnessing to Prayer

Show your students that prayer is important to you. This can't be overemphasized. If your school has a chapel, make a habit of visiting it and praying there. During study hall supervision or while proctoring a test, you might pray the rosary, which means you can still have an eye on the students. One of my indelible high school memories was the sight of my government teacher walking outside praying the rosary.

When a student is in need, do you ever say, "I'll pray for you"? Even better, pray for the student out loud on the spot. This can be an informal, spontaneous prayer or a formula prayer such as the Our Father. Having had the experience of being prayed for several times like this—even over the phone—I know how consoling and encouraging it can be.

Faculty Prayer

At one school in my area, the principal and faculty gathered in the principal's office every morning to pray together briefly. Your group could meet in a corner of the faculty room or in the chapel instead, and if not daily, meet once a week, perhaps on Monday mornings. Faculty could take turns leading the prayer session.

Faculty Meetings

Make a ten- or fifteen-minute prayer service an integral part of your monthly faculty meeting. Incorporating one or two questions for faith-sharing during each service helps build a sense of community. Teachers can take turns preparing the prayer services.

Faculty Retreat

Once a year it is good to gather as a faculty for a retreat, a time to pray together. This could be a half-day experience or as long as a weekend at a retreat house. The advantage of this experience is twofold: it will deepen the spiritual lives of the faculty and also nurture community.

Proof of Prayer

A joke making the rounds on the Internet is about a woman driver who is consumed with road rage when the car in front of her stops for a yellow light. She pounds the steering wheel, swears, and gestures in anger until a police officer taps on her window. He takes her to the police station where she is kept in a holding cell. When the police officer returns, he apologizes and explains, "When I saw your bumper stickers 'What would Jesus do?' 'Right to Life' and 'My child is an honor's student at St. John's school,' I assumed you were driving a stolen car."

The true test of our prayer is whether there is improvement in the way we live. Jesus taught, "Not everyone who says to me 'Lord, Lord' will enter the kingdom of heaven, but only the one who does the will of my Father in heaven" (Matthew 7:21).

Villagers called the spiritual mother of my community, St. Julie Billiart, "the walking love of God." What do your students and your coworkers call you? If your prayer life is strong and vibrant, your everyday actions and words will reflect this unconsciously. You will show the same love, compassion, and thirst for justice as the master teacher Jesus did.

An Encouraging Word

During my first year of teaching religion to ninth graders I felt like a dismal failure. The students constantly questioned and challenged what I said. In particular, I could count on one bright girl named Barbara to throw a monkey wrench into my well-planned lessons. A colleague advised me just to trust in the Holy Spirit to speak through me and teach the students in ways I was unaware of. So I went on in sheer faith. Then one day while correcting tests, I discovered this note Barbara had added to her essay: "Sister, you probably won't believe this, but I go to daily Mass and Communion. Something you said a while ago made me realize how important my faith is." This revelation was a special gift. Usually we never know how we affect our students' lives. We just keep on keeping on and doing our best, trusting in the Holy Spirit.

— 7 —

CELEBRATING THE LITURGICAL YEAR

Seasons of the liturgical year become more meaningful and memorable because of the traditions associated with them. Teach the traditions of Advent, Christmas, Lent, and Easter and carry them out in school. Hold assemblies or celebrate Mass for these seasons.

As a source for daily prayer you might use a book that offers prayers and reflections in keeping with the day's liturgy. Several of these books are listed in the chapter "Resources for Prayer" at the back of this book.

Visual Reinforcement

Decorate your classroom with a seasonal motif using items such as Advent wreaths, Mary candles, Jesse trees, Christmas cribs, alleluias, paschal candles, Easter eggs, as well as posters and art that reflect the season. If possible, dress to reflect the different seasons, for example, by wearing a Marian pin for Advent, the color purple for Lent, and Christmas and Easter earrings or pins.

Prayers

Pray prayers particular to each season: the "O Antiphons" during Advent, Christmas carols, the stations during Lent, and the *Regina Coeli* during the Easter season. Send home prayers related to the liturgical celebrations, for example, a Christmas tree blessing, a manger blessing, a lenten prayer, an Easter blessing, and for Pentecost a prayer to the Holy Spirit.

Advent Traditions

Your students could offer prayers and do good deeds for one another, a practice called Kris Kindl (Christ Child). They draw names to determine who their secret Kris Kindl will be.

Display and bless an Advent wreath, an evergreen wreath with four candles set in it. Three candles should be purple and one pink for the third Sunday, or use white candles with colored bows. Light the candles during the respective weeks of Advent, praying a prayer associated with each week's gospel.

→ See #16 on page 120 for the O Antiphons, which can be incorporated in your Advent observance.

Lent Traditions

This is the time for reconciliation celebrations and the stations of the cross. Your school might also plan a project or two to raise money or collect food for the poor. Encourage students to join in and support parish lenten activities.

→ See #17 on page 122 for the Stations of the Cross.

→ See #9 on page 101 for a penitential prayer service.

Food Linked to Seasons and Feasts

Distribute some of the foods associated with the religious seasons and discuss their meanings.

Lent: hot cross buns (a symbol of the crucifixion) and pretzels (that stand for praying hands)

Easter: jellybeans (the colors are symbolic), Easter eggs (new life: Christ emerging from the tomb), lamb cake (the paschal lamb)

Christmas: candy canes (originally a shepherd's crook, but a modern interpretation is that the J-shape is for Jesus, the white represents Christ's purity, the red the blood he shed, and the three red stripes the Holy Trinity)

Celebrating Feast Days

Observe Catholic feasts in a special way with a brief prayer service based on the feast or with a school-wide liturgy.

Other ways to celebrate include:

St. Nicholas Day, December 6: Give the children treats and little presents.

Epiphany: Hold a mission assembly with gifts (monetary or prayers) for the missions.

St. Valentine's Day, February 14: Tell the story of St. Valentine. Give cards or candy and other gifts to needy people.

St. Patrick's Day, March 17: Wear shamrocks and dress in green. Pray the "Breastplate of St. Patrick." (You can find this prayer on page 139.)

St. Joseph Day, March 19: Prepare a St. Joseph Shrine Table with flowers and bread shaped in forms. Collect food donations from stores or the school community. Invite all to share a meal at the table. Deliver the donated food to a food pantry.

Pentecost: Pray the Litany of the Holy Spirit near this feast. (This prayer can be found on page 123.)

St. Thérèse of Lisieux, October 1: She was known as the "Little Flower" and promised to send a shower of roses to earth, so display a rose in a vase.

St. Francis of Assisi, October 4: Encourage participation in a blessing of animals. Pray the "Prayer for Peace," which is attributed to St. Francis. (It is on page 135.)

Feast of All Saints: Hold a contest for all the families by sending home questions about the saints to be answered. Award a prize to the family that returns the sheet first with the correct answers. An alternate: Have the children dress up and process as "saints."

Marian feasts: Pray a decade of the rosary, the Litany of Loreto (on page 143), or another Marian prayer. Sing a Marian hymn.

Liturgy of the Hours

The Liturgy of the Hours, also called the Divine Office, is prayed daily by priests and women and men religious. Some religious communities, like the Trappists, pray all seven hours, getting up at midnight and early in the morning to do so. This is the official prayer of the Church, so all Christians are welcome to pray it, especially Morning and Evening Prayer (formerly called Matins and Vespers). The Liturgy of the Hours follows the seasons and feasts of the liturgical year, just as Mass does. For more on the Liturgy of the Hours, visit www.liturgyhours.org.

Introduce the students to a brief form of one of the hours. For example, you might pray morning prayer together to celebrate a certain occasion. Prepare them by giving them an outline, such as the one for Morning Prayer below.

You might also incorporate parts of the Prayer of Christians in your lessons. For example, end a lesson about Mary with the "intercessions" from the common of the Blessed Virgin Mary (see Web). Giving the students a taste of this prayer might whet their appetites for more.

> **MORNING PRAYER**
>
> *Lord, open my lips.* (Sign a cross on your lips.)
> *And my mouth shall proclaim your praise.*
> *Glory to...*
>
> Antiphon
> Psalm, Glory Be, short prayer
>
> Antiphon
> Canticle from Scripture, Glory Be, short prayer
>
> Antiphon
> Psalm, Glory Be, short prayer
>
> Reading from Scripture
> Responsory
>
> Antiphon
> Zechariah's Canticle (Benedictus)
> Antiphon repeated
>
> Intercessions
> Our Father
>
> Prayer of the day
> *May the Lord bless us, protect us from all evil, and bring us to everlasting life. Amen.*

— 8 —

TEACHING TRADITIONAL PRAYERS

Although the home is "the domestic church," in our largely secular culture we can't assume that children learn the basic Catholic prayers there. It falls upon us to teach the Our Father, the Hail Mary, and other traditional prayers, or at least reinforce them. By learning these time-honored prayers, children are able to pray together with other Catholics as the people of God. It also gives them words to express what is in their hearts when they turn to prayer.

Always explain prayers in class, phrase by phrase, before the children memorize them. Ideas for the Our Father can be found in the *Catechism of the Catholic Church,* in the fourth book from paragraphs 2777–2865.

Rewards are great motivators. Give a reward to children when they have mastered a prayer. This could be as simple as a name badge that says, "I learned the Our Father." Or you might make a chart and place a star after a child's name when he or she knows the prayer or prayers.

To save class time, arrange for a "prayer listener" (a parent or teacher aide) to hear individual children say the prayers in a corner of the room or in the hall.

Report back to the parents which prayers their child knows and those he or she still needs to master. That way the parents might be motivated to help the child.

Techniques for Prayer Practice

- Show the prayer on the board or screen and have the class repeat it as you erase a word or phrase at a time until the students are saying the entire prayer by heart.
- Write phrases of the prayer on strips and have children arrange them in order.
- Write phrases on puzzle pieces that the children put together as they pray the prayer. One giant puzzle can be assembled by the class, or each child can have his or her own puzzle.
- Make a transparency of a prayer leaving blanks for some words and have the children fill in the blanks.
- Make a large circle on sturdy paper and mark off pie-shaped sections. In each section write a phrase from a prayer. Attach a spinner to the center of the circle. The children spin the spinner, read the phrase it points to, and add the next phrase.
- Make two large circles. Divide one circle into pie-shaped sections and write phrases from a prayer in the sections. Out of the other circle cut a wedge the size of one of the sections. Use a brad to attach this circle on top of the whole one. Have the children turn the top circle to reveal each consecutive phrase of the prayer. They can also turn

the circle to sections at random and see if they can say the phrase that follows the revealed phrase.

- Print phrases from a prayer in mixed order along two sides of a card. Print the entire prayer on the back of the card. Along the sides of the card make a notch next to each phrase. Cut a length of yarn or string so that the children can wind it around the card, going from phrase to phrase in the order of the prayer. They can check their work using the back of the card.

- Write the phrases of a prayer on cards of one color and interpretations of phrases on cards of another color. Have the children match the cards.

- Divide a prayer into phrases and assign each one to a group of children. Have the group print the words on a sheet of paper and draw symbols or illustrations to go with them. When the pictures are finished, tape them together to make a banner to hang in your classroom.

- Have the children bring in six-inch boxes or cubes. Give them copies of the traditional prayers to paste on each side of the cube. Have the students take the prayer cubes home and use them to learn the prayers.

- Teach the children prayers using gestures or sign language. Or have them learn sung versions of the prayers.

The Rosary

The rosary is the prayer perhaps most associated with Catholicism. It is the prayer Mary asked us to pray in her various appearances on earth. When we pray the rosary, we unite two forms of prayer. While our minds dwell on the mysteries in the lives of Jesus and his mother (the Joyful, Luminous, Sorrowful, and

Glorious Mysteries), our lips say the prayers. Especially during the months of May, Mary's month, and October, the month of the rosary, you might want to share activities and instruction related to the rosary.

- Pray a decade together each day.
- Stage a living rosary.
- Display posters on the mysteries.
- Make rosaries and distribute them.
- Have students act out each mystery, dance it, or form a tableau of it.

→ See #10 on pages 102-107 for information on the rosary. For more information on the rosary, visit www.theholyrosary.org.

The Stations of the Cross

The stations, or way of the cross, allows people who can't travel to Jerusalem to trace the steps of Our Lord's passion and death. Here are a few ways to incorporate them in school:

- Pray the stations each Friday during Lent.
- Give the students stations booklets or have them write their own with reflections relating the stations to their own lives.
- Challenge the students to write a short poem for each station using a certain form, such as a cinquain (a five-line stanza).
- Present the stations in a unique way for the parish or students' families.

- Use audiovisuals to present the stations: posters, slides, etc.
- Visit a shrine that has outdoor stations.

→ See #17 on page 122 for a list of the stations of the cross. For more on the stations, visit www.catholic.org.

Catholic Prayer Practices

Familiarize your students with the following prayer practices:

- a novena: nine days of prayer (See #18 on page 123 for an example of a novena prayer: The Exaltation of the Holy Cross.)
- an octave: eight days of prayer
- a triduum: three days of prayer (See #12 on page 113 for a triduum retreat for the Holy Triduum.)
- a Holy Hour before the Blessed Sacrament (See page 146 for the Divine Praises usually prayed at Benediction.)
- veneration of a relic
- litanies (See #19 on page 123 for the Litany of the Holy Spirit.)

— 9 —

TEACHING SCRIPTURE-BASED PRAYERS

The Constitution on Divine Revelation (21) states: "In the sacred books the Father who is in heaven comes lovingly to meet his children and talks with them." If prayer is communing with God, what better way is there to enter into it than through God's Word? In the Bible God speaks directly to us, revealing himself as a loving God. Reading Scripture, then, is listening to God and thereby coming to know and love God. Moreover, the Bible is a goldmine of ready-made prayers that we can adapt to our situations. In addition, we can use any verses as a launching pad to God by savoring the words and letting them penetrate our hearts. When we introduce students to the treasures of the Bible, we give them the means to enrich their spiritual life abundantly.

Celebrate Scripture

Hold a ceremony to enthrone the Bible. Sing a song about God's Word, process with the Bible and candles, and then place the

Bible on a pillow on a special table or shelf. Include a reading about Scripture such as verses from Psalm 119 or Matthew 7:24–27, which is the parable of the house built on rock. Invite your students to approach the Bible individually to bow before it or lay their hand on it and pray, "Your word, O Lord, is a lamp for my feet" (Psalm 119:105).

As a culminating activity for a unit or as a celebration of a feast, season, or special time (like report card time), plan a prayer service that includes Scripture using this outline:

Opening Song
Introduction to the theme
Reading from Scripture
Psalm response
Quiet time
Prayer
Closing Song

→ See #6 on page 97 for a prayer service on Scripture.

Reading the Bible

Teach your students various ways to read the Bible:

- *Bit-by-bit* Read only one or two lines and sink into them, in imitation of Mary, the listening Virgin, who pondered God's word in her heart.
- *Book-by-book* Read a book of the Bible straight through.
- *One track* Read according to a theme such as prayer, faith, forgiveness, or justice. Use a concordance or other index to find references.
- *Methodical* Read the Bible from beginning to end.
- *Liturgical* Read the readings for the day's eucharistic celebration.

- *Lucky dip* Open the Bible at random and read.
- *Father David Knight's method* Keep the Bible on your pillow and every night read just one verse. You can always read one verse. Some nights you might read three or four. Before you know it, you'll have read an entire book.

At times offer your students the opportunity for quiet reading and praying over Scripture. Go with them into your parish church and invite them to spread out as far from one another as possible. Let them read passages at random or provide them with a study guide for a particular theme or passage.

LECTIO DIVINA

Lectio divina, or sacred reading, originated with the Benedictine monks. It has four steps that have been compared to Jacob's ladder, which stretched into heaven, because ultimately this method leads to union with God. Although *lectio divina* is usually associated with reading Scripture, it can be used for other spiritual reading and even for reading the experiences of our lives. Here are the steps.

1. *Lectio* (reading)

Choose a passage from Scripture. Read until an idea attracts you. The words will jump out at you.

2. *Meditatio* (meditating)

Stop and mull over the idea that struck you. Repeat the words over and over and let them sink into your heart and mind. Delve into the meaning of the words and savor them. Think about why these words attract you. When it dawns on you, move into the next step.

3. *Oratio* (praying)

This step takes you from the head to the heart. Respond with a prayer as the words prompt you: a prayer of adoration, thanksgiving, sorrow for sin, petition, or love. Stay with these feelings. Let yourself desire God. Put yourself at the disposal of God's Spirit, preparing for God's action. At this point you may return to the passage and continue reading, or you might be lifted into the next step.

4. *Contemplatio* (contemplating)

Be with God, enjoying his presence and letting him love you. Be alone with God in the great silence that is too deep for words. Here God takes over your faculties and assumes the lead. It may seem as though nothing is happening, but this is deceptive. Zen wisdom applies to this step: "Sitting still/ doing nothing, spring comes and the grass grows by itself."

You may repeat steps several times or just do one step. When you are distracted or can't sustain the prayer, go back to the passage and read it until another word or phrase strikes you.

Your students can be taught *lectio divina* in small groups. Light a candle to recall God's presence. Guide the groups through this process:

1. In each group one person reads a passage while the rest listen. Then another person reads the passage because people read with different intonations, uncovering different meanings.

2. Allow time for a word or phrase to touch everyone's heart.
3. Invite the students to reflect aloud. Explain that reflecting differs from discussing. In this case, each person shares thoughts without any response from the others. Some may simply share the word or phrase that has meaning for them.
4. Play a related song.
5. Invite the students to make a prayer response aloud, one or two simple sentences that Scripture prompts them to pray.
6. Sit in silence for a time.

The Psalms

The Book of Psalms is the prayer book of the Bible. The one hundred and fifty prayers in this book are three thousand years old and are prayed by Christians, Jews, and Muslims. Familiarize your students with these prayers, which Jesus, like all Jews, prayed every day. Use the footnotes and commentaries in your Bible to help you explain the meaning of the psalms. Explain to children that the psalms express all the feelings of our hearts: praise, thanksgiving, contrition, lament, and love. Tell them that the psalms are poetry, so they have repetition and imagery. When praying them it helps to visualize the image. Because the psalms were originally sung, incorporate musical versions of them into your prayer sessions. A moving prayer service can be created by including psalm verses accompanied by beautiful nature scenes flashed on a screen.

Singing Scripture

Many hymns are based on Scripture passages. Usually a line of print under the hymns in your parish hymnal gives their source. Weave these scriptural hymns into your lessons and prayer services.

Reflecting on Scripture

St. Teresa of Avila said, "We have such a great God that a single of his words contains thousands of secrets." Teach the students to pray over just one verse of Scripture. Direct them to consider the literal meaning, reflect on its meaning with them, and then speak to God about it. They might write their reflections and share them.

Receiving a Love Note

To let students experience God giving them a personal message, have a Scripture verse on a slip of paper delivered to them using one of these means:

- Put the papers folded in half in a bag or a box, perhaps a heart-shaped candy box. Pass around the container, having each student draw out a verse.
- Curl paper slips using the edge of a scissor blade. Attach one end of each slip inside the outline of a tree or heart or flowers and have the students pluck them.
- Insert the verses into balloons and inflate the balloons. Have the students take a balloon and burst it to retrieve the verse. Or write the verses on inflated balloons, deflate the balloons, and then let each student take one to inflate and read.

- Insert the papers into fortune cookies, purchased or homemade. These scripture fortune cookies can sometimes be found ready-made in religious goods stores. Or roll the papers and insert them in bugle-shaped snacks.

→ See #20 on page 125 for a list of appropriate Scripture verses.

Personalizing Scripture

Have the students paraphrase prayers in the Bible, such as the Magnificat or one of the psalms. Psalm 23 works well for this. Invite students to choose an image of God other than a shepherd, for example: counselor, leader, hero, friend.

Some psalms are acrostics, that is, each verse begins with a consecutive letter of the Hebrew alphabet. Invite your students to imitate the acrostic psalms and write a prayer using the letters of the alphabet or the letters in their names.

Read passages of the Bible to your students, or have them read the passages, inserting their names in them or substituting their names for pronouns. Ephesians 1:3–14 with this adaptation is very moving. The hymn to love in 1 Corinthians 13:4–7 makes a good examination of conscience if a person's name is substituted for the word "love."

Memorizing Verses

Pope John Paul II stated that "The blossoms…of faith and piety do not grow in the desert places of a memoryless catechesis" (*Catechesis in Our Time*, 55). Memorized Scripture verses will come to mind when they are needed. Encourage your students to "bank prayers." Share with them these techniques for memorizing verses:

- Reflect on the verse's meaning. Use a dictionary for unfamiliar words.
- Post a verse of the week on a refrigerator or mirror.
- Write the verse several times.
- Sing the verse to a tune.
- Make up motions to do as you say the verse.
- If the verse is long, memorize one section at a time.
- Memorize right before you go to bed. The words will stay in your mind better.

In class help your students memorize through these activities:
- Have the students put each letter of a verse on tagboard, cut it into puzzle pieces, and put the pieces in an envelope. Let them trade envelopes, put the puzzles together, and memorize the verses.
- Let them throw a ball, beanbag, or stuffed animal to one another. Each student who receives the item must recite a chosen verse or the next word of a verse.
- Letter, or have the students letter, verses on index cards. Keep the cards in a box or pocket for the students to study.
- Each week have a verse to be memorized posted or written on the board.

— 10 —

TEACHING MEDITATION

One day I led my ninth graders through a meditation on a gospel story. The next day as the students filed into class, one asked, "Can we do a meditation again?" Others chimed in, saying how much they liked that experience. I was surprised, but then I realized they had probably never meditated before and enjoyed the quiet time focusing on Jesus.

There are different methods for using the imagination to facilitate prayer. In his journal, the poet William Wordsworth recorded that when he was in a beautiful place, he often imagined Jesus next to him, for example, when he wrote his poem about daffodils, "I Wandered Lonely as a Cloud." Here are a few ways to lead students into meditation.

Begin by quieting the students down. Have them do a breathing exercise or pay attention to silence. They might mentally say their name over and over as if God is calling them. Little children can make the Sign of the Cross on their foreheads over and over until Jesus is in their minds.

Being with Jesus

Invite your students to imagine Jesus sitting next to them or on an empty chair in their room. Tell them to speak to him and imagine what he says in reply. Encourage them to do this in their rooms at home and speak to Jesus aloud. Another method is to have them imagine a room furnished to suit their taste. Perhaps it has a rocking chair, a fireplace, a view of mountains from the window. Invite them to go into this room and meet Jesus there. Or they can imagine meeting him at the seashore, in a garden, or on a mountaintop.

Tell younger children to imagine that they are in the crowd of children who run to Jesus, or that they are sitting next to him in a boat, or walking down a road with him. Invite them to tell him whatever is in their hearts.

Once I was in an audience of a thousand people when Father George Maloney, SJ., took us in an imaginary elevator down into the depths of our hearts. He slowly called out the floors as we descended, then left us in silence to commune with God. Sister Mary Therese Donze, ASC, leads children to pray "in their heart room" where God is. She bases her meditations on an object or picture and guides the children this way:

1. Consider the characteristics and uses of the object.
2. Reflect on the object relating it to life.
3. Have a conversation with Jesus in the quiet of your heart.

→ See #21 on page 128 for an example of leading children to pray in their "heart room."

St. Teresa of Avila recommended that we experience the Risen Lord by imagining that he is by our side all during the day. We can communicate with him every so often, with or without words.

Praying Memories

Invite your students to recall a time when they experienced God's love for them in a special way, when they felt close to God. Have them recall the place, the details of what happened, and how they felt. Then tell them to re-live that event in their imagination. Finally, have them speak to God about it.

Using Imagination

Encourage the students to visualize the people or situations they are praying for. A vivid picture in their minds will make their prayer more intense.

Ignatian Meditation

In his *Spiritual Exercises*, St. Ignatius of Loyola taught this form of meditation using a gospel event.

- Ask for a particular grace.
- Use your imagination and all five senses to fill in the details of the gospel setting, see the characters and hear them speak, and watch the action. How do you feel toward Jesus in the scene? Replay the event in your mind as if you were participating. For instance, as you meditate on the Nativity, Mary might let you hold the newborn baby for a while.
- Then discuss the event with Jesus.

Guided Meditation

Here is a method for leading your students into a gospel event and having them link it to their lives.

- Settle the students down. Have them quiet their bodies and minds.
- Read a gospel story. Supply helpful background information. Then tell the story adding details such as the weather, the setting, and the expressions on people's faces. Make comments that bring the story to life. For example, in telling about Zacchaeus, mention that Jesus knew he was in the tree, and Jesus also knew the secrets of his heart. In the story of the cure of the blind Bartimaeus, ask what the first thing was that Bartimaeus saw.
- Pose questions based on the story that compel the students to draw meaning for their own lives.
- Allow time for quiet reflection on the questions.

→ See #22 on page 129 for a sample guided meditation on Zacchaeus.

Fantasy Prayer

Create a symbolic situation in which the students imagine themselves present. Invite them to make choices, act and react, and then analyze their feelings. For example, they can imagine that they meet Jesus along a path and he gives them a gift. What will he give them? Why? How do they react? Or have them imagine themselves as they were as a baby in a crib. What did the room look like? What did they look like? What were they doing? How do they feel about this baby?

— 11 —

TEACHING CENTERING PRAYER

Long ago in France, St. John Vianney, also known as the Curé d'Ars, noticed that an old man spent hours in the parish church. The peasant would sit motionless, doing nothing. Finally one day the priest asked him, "What are you doing when you sit here?" The man replied, "I look at him and he looks at me." The man was contemplating.

Contemplation is simply resting in God, peacefully placing your attention on God and letting God work in you. The word comes from the Latin *con*, which means "with" and the word for "temple." To contemplate is to be with God in a sacred place, in the temple. In this case, the temple is ourselves.

There are a few ways to enter into a contemplative state and "look at" God beyond thoughts and images. Share them with your students.

- Keep silent and become aware of your mind. What is revealed to you?
- Become aware of body sensations. Move from one part of

your body to another, becoming conscious of the sensations in it.

- Become aware of your breathing. Be aware of the air as it passes through your nostrils. Realize that the air you are breathing is filled with the presence of God. As you breathe, you are drawing God in.
- Become aware of the sounds around you. Be aware of your power to hear. Realize that God is sounding all around you.
- Take a familiar object and hold it. Use all your senses to become fully aware of it.
- Sit a while now silently gazing at God.

The Basis for Centering Prayer

Centering prayer is founded on the belief that God dwells within us. St. John of the Cross said, "O soul, most beautiful of Creatures who longs to know where the beloved is, you yourself are the very tabernacle where he dwells." Centering prayer is merely loving attention to God dwelling within us. It has its roots in the prayer tradition of the church fathers and desert fathers and incorporates the prayer techniques of the Eastern Church.

The Steps of Centering Prayer

- Quiet down. Sit upright so your head is well supported by your spine. Keep your eyes gently closed so energy is not wasted by what you see. To relax, breathe slowly three times: exhale, take in fresh air, hold it, exhale.
- Move toward God within you. Think only of God who is living deep within you and ponder God's love for you. Be

present to God. Let God's overwhelming love and goodness attract you. Rest in God's presence.
- Respond with a word or phrase, such as "I love you," "My Lord and my God," or "Jesus." Repeat this "prayer word" slowly in your mind.
- Attend to God and enjoy God's presence. When you know you are aware of things other than God, use your prayer word to bring you back. Don't stop to think about how you're doing. Focus on giving God your loving attention.
- At the end, pray a prayer. Use the Our Father or another prayer to make the transition out of centering prayer back to the world around you.

Before and after Centering Prayer

Explain the prayer to the students and have them choose a prayer word. Then guide them through the prayer with these words:

> Sit straight and still. Close your eyes and think only of God dwelling deep within you. Think of God's great love for you. Pray with me: "Jesus, I believe that you are present in the center of my being, loving me. In these next few minutes I want to remember that I am all yours. Let me come into your presence. Draw me to yourself, Jesus." Remain still. Repeat your prayer word in your mind. Stay with Jesus who loves you.

After the prayer experience, you might ask the students to write their responses to it. Let students respond orally if they choose to. Encourage them to practice centering prayer at home.

→ See #23 page 131 for a skit that introduces students to centering prayer.

— 12 —

TEACHING MANTRAS

A mantra is a short prayer—a word, phrase, or sentence—that is prayed repeatedly. Sometimes it is called prayer of the heart. Mantras have a long history. Early Christian hermits prayed them to stay anchored in God. Monks in Egypt continually prayed, "O God, come to my assistance."

I discovered mantras on my own. One Christmas Day my sister called with the news that our father had had a heart attack and had already been anointed. I rushed to the hospital where Dad was lying unconscious. Tubes were connected to him, and a respirator was hissing away. This crisis was especially frightening because no one in our family had ever been seriously ill before. That night I couldn't sleep. All of a sudden I found myself saying the words "The Lord is my shepherd" from Psalm 23 over and over. The words echoed in my heart and calmed me with a sense of God's presence. Eventually I slept. The next morning when I returned to my father's hospital room I was introduced to a male nurse who had worked overtime throughout Christmas night caring for him. To my astonishment, the nurse's name was Bob Shepard. And, yes, my dad recovered from this heart attack.

When are too tired, too weak, or too distressed to pray from a prayer book or to formulate our own prayers, we can pray a mantra. This simple way of praying has power to bring us relief and rest and to open us to God. Its repetition is as soothing as the motion of a rocking chair, a swing, or the waves on the shore. The rhythm imitates our breathing and our heartbeats. Praying mantras is like a child incessantly crying, "Mommy, I need you," or a lover tirelessly repeating, "I love you."

Ways to Pray Mantras

Mantras can be prayed anytime, not just in emergencies. It's especially helpful to pray them while waiting for something or while doing a monotonous task. Mantras can be prayed anywhere: in a checkout line, in an airport, in a doctor's office, or in a car. There are various ways to pray them: silently, aloud, singing them, or synchronizing them with your breathing. Some people like to keep track of mantras with rosary beads.

As you pray a mantra, a word might change, altering the meaning of your prayer. For example, as you pray, "I love you, O Lord, my strength" (Psalm 18:1), you might find that you are praying "my savior" instead of "my strength."

Although mantras can be prayed while walking, running, swimming, or any other activity, it is recommended that you sit relaxed with hands resting on your lap. Close your eyes and breathe deeply, letting all tension flow out of your body and mind. Focus on the Lord dwelling in you and then whisper the verse slowly over and over, listening with love and desire.

> **SOURCES OF MANTRAS**
>
> The Book of Psalms is a wonderful source of mantras. They can be gleaned from other Bible books as well. See Isaiah 25:1; Isaiah 64:8; Habakkuk 3:2; Luke 1:47; John 6:68; and 1 Timothy 1:17. Mantras can also be taken from the Mass prayers, prayers of saints, or other favorite prayers.
>
> Some mantras are reverse mantras, that is, rather than words we say to God, they are words that God is saying to us. For example, "Do not be afraid" (Matthew 28:5). Other examples are Isaiah 41:13; Isaiah 43:1; Matthew 28:20; John 11:25; John 16:33; and 2 Corinthians 12:9.

A Favorite Mantra

Some saints had favorite short prayers. St. Francis of Assisi often prayed, "My God and my all." Before St. Catherine of Siena died, for forty days straight she repeated, "I have sinned. Have mercy on me." St. Teresa of Avila revealed that during a sickness she clung to the words "We accept good things from God; and should we not accept evil?" (Job 2:10).

The Jesus Prayer

The Eastern Church gave us the Jesus Prayer, which dates back at least to the fifth century. This prayer is repeated continuously and leads to union with God: "Jesus Christ, Son of God, have mercy on me, a sinner." Teach your students this mystical prayer. It can be prayed inhaling on the first half and exhaling on the second half.

Taizé Prayer

The monks of Taizé, an ecumenical, international community in France, have made chanted mantras popular. Their prayer sessions are a combination of sung mantras, Scripture, and silence. Their website has this explanation of the short songs:

> Using just a few words, they express a basic reality of faith, quickly grasped by the mind. As the words are sung over many times, this reality gradually penetrates the whole being. Meditative singing thus becomes a way of listening to God.

RESOURCES FOR PRAYER

The following list contains recent books that are still available from publishers. Other books, including classics on prayer, can be found in libraries or on the Internet.

Prayers for School and Classroom

McNally, Thomas and William George Storey. *Day by Day: The Notre Dame Prayerbook for Students.* Ave Maria Press, 2004.

Donze, Mary Terese, ASC. *In My Heart Room: 21 Love Prayers for Children.* Liguori, 1998.

Foley, Kathleen and Peggy O'Leary. *Daily Prayers in the Classroom: Interactive Daily Prayer.* Liturgical Press, 2002. (Contains a brief reflection with questions for children for every day of the year.)

Hiesberger, Jean Marie and Maureen Gallagher. *Take Ten: Daily Bible Reflections for Teens,* Lectionary-based. St. Mary's Press, 2004.

Kenny-Sheputis, Christine. *Take Me Home: Notes on the Church Year for Children.* Liturgy Training Publications, 1992. (Contains handouts for the seasons and feast days of the year.)

Koch, Carl. *Prayers by Teenagers: Dreams Alive.* St. Mary's Press, 1991.

———. *More Dreams Alive: Prayers by Teenagers.* St. Mary's Press, 1995.

Krupp, Laure, Matt Miller, and Mary Shrader. *The Catholic Youth Prayer Book.* St. Mary's Press, 2006.

Mazar, Peter. *Take Me Home, Too: More Notes for the Church Year.* Liturgy Training Publications. 1999. (Contains handouts for the seasons and feast days of the year.)

Jeep, Elizabeth McMahon. *Blessings and Prayers through the Year: A Resource for School and Parish* (with two music CDs) Liturgy Training Publications, 2004.

Snyder, Bernadette McCarver. *Paper Bag Prayers: Finding God in Little Things, Any Time, Any Place.* Liguori, 2006.

Tassi, Filomena and Peter. *500 Prayers for Catholic Schools and Parish Youth Groups.* Twenty-Third Publications, 2004.

Verhalen, Philip A. *Prayers for the Classroom.* Liturgical Press, 1998. (Prayers used to begin high school classes, arranged by month with a thematic index.)

Lewis, Suzanne. *Children's Daily Prayer 2007–2008.* Liturgy Training Publications, 2006. (Issued annually.)

Guides for Teaching Prayer

Berger, Alison. *The Prayer Journey.* Jump Starts for Catechist Series. Twenty-Third Publications, 2005.

Costello, Gwen. *Praying with Children.* Jump Starts for Catechists Series. Twenty-Third Publications, 2007.

———. *Prayer Primer for Catechists and Teachers*. Twenty-Third Publications, 1998.

Gallagher, Maureen. *Praying with Young People: Tips for Catechists*. Paulist Press, 2007.

Hall, Thelma, RC. *Too Deep for Words: Rediscovering Lectio Divina*. Paulist Press, 1998.

Pennington, M. Basil. *An Invitation to Centering Prayer*. Liguori, 2001.

———. *Centered Living: The Way of Centering Prayer*. Liguori, 1999.

Prayer Services and Retreats

Berger, Alison. *Growing in Grace: 35 Prayer Services for Children*. Twenty-Third Publications, 2005.

Hakowski, Maryann M. *22 Ready Made Prayer Services with 100 Extra Prayer Ideas*. St. Mary's Press, 2006.

Costello, Gwen. *Junior High Prayer Services by Themes and Season*. Twenty-Third Publications, 2000.

McCann, Deborah. *Let Us Gather: Prayer Services for Catholic Schools and Assemblies*. Twenty-Third Publications, 2002.

Regan, S. Kevin. *Opening Doors of Truth and Love: Teen Prayer Services*. Twenty-Third Publications, 2005.

———. *Twenty More Teen Prayer Services*. Twenty-Third Publications, 1996.

———. *Teen Prayer Services: 20 Themes for Reflection and Prayer*. Twenty-Third Publications, 1996.

Schneider, Sr. M. Valerie. *Weekly Prayer Services for Teens*. 3 Vol.: Years A, B (1996); Years B, C (1997); Years C, A (1998). Twenty-Third Publications.

Vankat, Jennie. *Seasonal Retreats and Prayer Services for Young Adolescents*. St. Mary's Press, 2007.

Prayer Lessons

Wezeman, Phyllis and Jude Dennis Fournier. *Twenty More Prayer Lessons for Children.* Twenty-Third Publications, 1997.

———. *Twenty Prayer Lessons for Children.* Twenty-Third Publications, 1996.

Meditation Books

Costello, Gwen. *Praying the Stations with Children.* Twenty-Third Publications, 2000.

———. *Praying the Stations with Teenagers.* Twenty-Third Publications, 2000.

Egeberg, Gary. *Stations for Teens: Meditations on the Death and Resurrection of Jesus.* St. Mary's Press, 2000.

Haas, David. *Prayers before an Awesome God: The Psalms for Teenagers.* St. Mary's Press, 1998.

Reehorst, Jane, B.V.M. *Guided Meditations for Children: How to Teach Children to Pray Using Scripture.* Harcourt Religious Publishers, 2000. (Using their five senses in line with Ignatian meditation, children set a scriptural scene as a backdrop for prayer.)

Schneider, M. Valerie, S.N.D. *Gospel Scenes for Teens: 23 Guided Prayer Meditations.* Twenty-Third Publications, 2000.

Prayer Programs

Braden-Whartenby, Geri and Joan Finn Connelly. *One-Day Retreats for Junior High Youth.* St. Mary's Press, 1997.

———. *One-Day Retreats for Senior High Youth.* St. Mary's Press, 1997.

Hakowski, Maryann. *Youth Retreats for Any Schedule.* St. Mary's Press, 2007. (Five retreats on various topics related to young people.)

———. *Getaways with God: Youth Retreats for Any Schedule* St. Mary's Press, 2003. (Five retreats for senior high: a weekend, a day, or a few hours.)

Kurtz, Dennis. *Youth Engaging Scripture: Diving into the Sunday Gospels.* St. Mary's Press, 2007. (Also on CD-ROM.)

Perrotta, Kevin and Gerald Darring. *Six Weeks with the Bible for Catholic Teens: Exploring God's Word.* Loyola Press. (Each guide has six sessions containing Scripture text and questions that relate it to their lives.)

Yes! Congress. St. Mary's Press. (Training for teens and adult mentors to lead Bible sharing.)

Books about Prayer

Bloom, Archbishop Anthony. *Beginning to Pray.* Paulist Press, 1982.

Jungmann, Joseph A. *Christian Prayer through the Centuries.* Paulist Press, 2008.

Glavich, Mary Kathleen, S.N.D. *The Catholic Companion to the Psalms.* ACTA Publications, 2008.

———. *Prayer Moments for Every Day of the Year.* E.T. Nedder Publishing, 2008.

———. *The Rosary: The Gospel on Beads.* E.T. Nedder Publishing, 2004.

Green, Thomas H., S.J. *Opening to God: A Guide to Prayer.* Ave Maria Press, 2006.

Halpin, Marlene, O.P. *189 Ways to Contact God: Find the Prayer Starter That Works for You.* Loyola Press, 1999.

Prayer Books for Teachers

Caruso, Michael P., S.J., ed. *Stay with Us, Lord: Prayer and Reflections for Educators*. NCEA, 2005.

Costello, Gwen. *A Prayerbook for Catechists*. Twenty-Third Publications, 2001.

Farry, Ginger. *A Teacher's Prayerbook*. Twenty-Third Publications, 1999.

Kealey, Robert J. *The Prayer of Catholic Educators*, NCEA, 2003.

Lucinio, Jeanette. *Prayers for Catechists*. Liturgy Training Publications. 2001.

— *Appendix 1* —

ADDITIONAL PRAYERS AND ACTIVITIES

1. JESUS TEACHES PRAYER (for page 11)

Direct the students to look up and read the following Scripture references.

How Jesus prays	Matthew 11:25; Mark 1:35; Mark 6:41; Luke 4:16; Luke 6:12; Luke 22:31–32; Luke 22:39–42
Jesus praying at important times in his life	Mark 14:36; Luke 3:21–22; Luke 6:12–13; Luke 9:28–29; Luke 23:34, 46; John 17:1–26
Jesus' teachings on prayer	Matthew 6:5–6; Matthew 6:8; Matthew 7:21; Luke 11:5–8; Luke 11:9; Luke 18:9–14; John 16:23

2. THE OUR FATHER (for page 11)

To enrich your own background, read part four of the *Catechism of the Catholic Church*, which presents a thorough explanation of the Our Father.

Use the following reflection with your students to call attention to the meaning of the words of the Our Father and to reinforce the idea that in prayer we are really speaking to God.

■ ■ ■

Our Father, Who art in heaven.

Yes?

Don't interrupt me. I'm praying.

But you called me!

Called you? No, I didn't call you. I'm praying. Our Father who art in Heaven.

There, you did it again.

Did what?

Called me. You said, "Our Father, who art in Heaven." Well, here I am. What's on your mind?

But I didn't mean anything by it. I was, you know, just saying my prayers for the day. I always say the Lord's Prayer. It makes me feel good, kind of like fulfilling a duty.

Well, all right. Go on.

Okay. Hallowed be thy name.

Hold it right there. What do you mean by that?

It means…good grief. How in the world should I know? It's just a part of the prayer. By the way, what does it mean?

It means honored, holy, wonderful.

Ah, that makes sense. Thanks. Thy kingdom come, Thy will be done, on earth as it is in Heaven.

Do you really mean that?

Sure, why not?

What are you doing about it?

Doing? Why, nothing, I guess. I just think it would be good if you got control of everything down here like you have up there. We're kind of in a mess down here you know.

Yes, I know; but have I got control of you?

Well, I go to church.

That isn't what I asked you. What about your bad temper? You've really got a problem there, you know. And what about some of the language you use and the stuff you talk about? What about thinking you're better than others? What about the people you've judged? Remember, that's my job, not yours.

Now hold on just a minute! Stop picking on me! I'm just as good as some of the rest of those people at church!

Excuse me? I thought you were praying for MY will to be done? If that is to happen, it will have to start with the ones who are praying for it...like you, for example.

Oh, all right. I guess I do have some issues. Now that you mention it, I could probably name some others.

So could I.

I haven't thought about it very much until now, but I really would like to cut out some of those things. I would like to...you know, be really free.

Good. Now we're getting somewhere. We'll work together, you and I. I'm proud of you.

Look, Lord, I need to finish up here. Give us this day our daily bread.

You need to cut out some of the bread. You're a little overweight.

Hey, wait a minute! What is this? Here I am doing my religious duty, and all of a sudden you break in and remind me of all my problems.

Praying is a dangerous thing. You could end up changed. That's what I'm trying to bring across to you. Remember, you called me, and here I am. Keep praying.

I'm scared to.

Scared? Of what?

I know what you'll say.

Try me and see.

Forgive us our sins as we forgive those who sin against us.

What about Susan and others who have done you wrong?

See, I knew you would bring her up! Why, Lord? She's told lies about me and spread stories. She never paid back the money she owes me. I've sworn to get even with her!

But what about your prayer?

I didn't, you know, really mean it.

Well, at least you're honest. But it's quite a load carrying around all that resentment, isn't it?

Yes, but I'll feel better as soon as I get even with her. Boy, have I got plans for her. She'll wish she had never been born!

No, you won't feel any better. You'll feel worse. Revenge isn't sweet. You know how unhappy you are. Well, I can change that.

You can? How?

> *Forgive Susan. Then I'll forgive you. And the hate and sin will be Susan's problem, not yours.*

OK. I know you're right. You always are. And more than I want revenge, I want to be right with you. *(sigh)* All right, all right. I forgive her.

> *There now! Wonderful! How do you feel?*

Hmm. Well, not bad. In fact, I feel pretty good! You know, I don't think I'll be going to bed all uptight tonight. I haven't been getting much sleep lately.

> *I know. But you're not through with your prayer, are you? Go on.*

Oh, all right. And lead us not into temptation, but deliver us from evil.

> *Good! Good! I'll do that. Just don't put yourself in a place where you can be tempted.*

What do you mean by that?

> *You know what I mean.*

Yeah, I know.

> *OK. Go ahead and finish your prayer.*

For thine is the kingdom, and the power, and the glory forever. Amen.

> *Do you know what would bring me glory and what would really make me happy?*

No, but I would like to know. I want to please you. I've really made a mess of things. I want to truly follow you. I can see now how great that would be. So tell me, how do I make you happy?

> *You just did.*

—Author Unknown

3. A PRAYER LAB (for page 23)

Activities should be geared to the age of the students. Here is a sample for junior high or high school age students.

Station 1

Contents A picture of Jesus.

Directions Art is a springboard for prayer. In silence look at this picture and let Jesus speak to your heart. Respond to him as you feel moved to do.

Station 2

Contents A few Bibles and a recording of an explanation of different reasons for praying.

Directions Listen to the tape and then find verses from the psalms that reflect these reasons.

Station 3

Contents A rosary and a chart of how to pray the rosary with a list of the mysteries.

Directions Study the chart and memorize one set of mysteries.

Station 4

Contents Copies of a gospel story.

Directions Read the story and then replay it in your mind putting yourself in the story. Imagine what people looked like, where they were, and their expressions. Then speak to Jesus about what happened.

Station 5

Contents Hymnals.

Directions Choose two hymns and analyze them. What do the words mean? What kind of prayers are they? When would you sing them?

Station 6
>*Contents* A list of one-line prayers such as:
>>Jesus;
>>My God, I love you;
>>My Lord and my God;
>>My Jesus, mercy;
>>My God and my all;
>>Jesus, for you I live.
>
>*Directions* Choose a prayer. Sit still and repeat the prayer over and over focusing on God dwelling in your heart.

4. EXAMINATION OF CONSCIENCE ON PRAYER (for page 25)

Prepare a leaflet that the students can use to form the habit of daily prayer. These are possible questions to include:

In the morning do I…
>say good morning to the Lord?
>thank and praise God for another day?
>pray the Morning Offering?
>ask God's help in making decisions?
>pray for the grace to do the right things and avoid sin?

During the day do I…
>think of God?
>pray grace before and after meals?
>turn to God in times of trouble?
>ask God's help?
>see God in others?
>pray during free moments?
>thank and praise God when I see one of God's gifts?

In the evening do I…
    think over the events of the day?
    ask God to bless my family, relatives, and friends?
    pray for people who need help?
    thank God for the good things that happened during the day?
    express sorrow for my failures to love?
    ask God to help me to be a better Christian tomorrow?

During the month do I…
    pray with the church?
    participate at Mass?
    join in special parish prayer times?
    read the Bible?
    pray the rosary and the stations of the cross?
    take time for personal prayer?
    spend extra time with the Lord?
    pray prayers such as the Hail Mary, the Our Father, and the Glory Be?
    pray my favorite prayers?

5. JOURNALING (for page 30)

Here are lines to help students get started with journaling:

    I feel like a success/failure when…
    I like/dislike…
    I wish…
    I don't care if…
    The best thing about me is…
    I am happy/sad when…

Nothing is as important to me as…
My favorite gospel story is…
I thank God especially for…
In the future I hope to be…
If you could be somebody else, who would you be?
How important in your life is religion?
What do you think is your chief fault?
What do you get most excited about?
What emotions are you feeling right now?
What name would you choose to describe yourself?
What person would you like to take a trip with?
What is your favorite place in the world?
What book has had an impact on your life?
What is your favorite movie?

6. SCRIPTURE PRAYER SERVICE
(for pages 31, 65)

THE GIFT OF GOD'S WORD

Song "Speak, Lord, I'm Listening" or other appropriate hymn

(Process with the Bible and place it on a special stand.)

Leader O good and loving God, we thank you for the gift of your Word. Through Scripture you reveal yourself to us, especially in the gospels where we meet Jesus, the Word made flesh. In Scripture you speak to us, telling us of your love for us and teaching us the way to happiness. May we always cherish your Word and follow it with all our hearts.

First Reading Isaiah 55:10–11 (God's word is fruitful.)

Psalm 119 (alternate sides)

Side 1 Your word, O Lord, endures forever; it is as firm as the heavens (v. 89).

Side 2 My heart stands in awe of your words (v. 161).

Side 1 I rejoice at your word like one who finds great spoil (v. 162).

Side 2 I trust in your word (v. 42).

Side 1 Your word is a lamp to my feet and a light to my path (v. 105).

Side 2 I hold back my feet from every evil way, in order to keep your word (v. 101).

Side 1 I treasure your word in my heart (v. 11).

Side 2 I will not forget your word (v. 16).

Side 1 I hope in your word (v. 81).

Side 2 Be good to your servant that I may live and observe your words (v. 17).

Side 1 The sum of your word is truth (v. 160).

Side 2 Of your kindness, O Lord, the earth is full (v. 64).

Reading Matthew 7:24–27 (The two houses)

TIME FOR REFLECTION

Response *Lord, hear our prayer.*

May we take time to listen to your Word…

May we always have hearts open to your Word…

May we understand your Word more and more…

May we live according to your Word…

May we bring others to your Word…

May we always love your Word…

Song A hymn of thanks and praise

7. SAMPLE SCHOOL PRAYER (for page 38)

The following is the school prayer of Incarnate Word Academy in St. Louis, Missouri (used here with permission).

We praise your name
 Lord Jesus Christ,
 Incarnate Word of God.
By your incarnation
 you dignified us.
Open our eyes
 that we may recognize you
 in one another.
Help us, O God,
 to be the loving presence of
 Jesus,
 the Incarnate Word,
 TODAY!

Praised be the Incarnate Word!
Forever! Amen!

8. LITURGY PLANNING GUIDE (for page 37)

Opening hymn: _____

First reading: _____
Read by: _____

Responsorial psalm: _____ ❏ recited
                                            ❏ sung

Gospel acclamation: _____ ❏ recited
                                            ❏ sung

Gospel reading: _____

General Intercessions read by: _____

Procession with gifts: wine: _____
                      hosts: _____
                      other: _____

Hymn: _____

Holy, Holy: _____ ❏ recited
                                          ❏ sung

Memorial acclamation: _____ ❏ recited
                                          ❏ sung

Great Amen: ❏ recited
             ❏ sung

Our Father: _____ ❏ recited
                                          ❏ sung

Sign of peace: _____

Communion hymn: _____

Thanksgiving: _____ ❏ recited
                                          ❏ sung
❏ silent   ❏ other: _____

Closing hymn: _____

9. PENITENTIAL PRAYER SERVICE
(for pages 40, 55)

CHANGING HEARTS OF STONE
(Give each student a stone that represents a hard heart. Place a pail before a crucifix.)

1. **Song** (Suggestions: "Hosea," "Jesus, Heal Us," "Remember Your Love")

2. **Prayer** *Holy Spirit, open our eyes to see how we have failed to love like Jesus. Open our hearts so that we are truly sorry for our sins for which Jesus died on the cross. Help us to make up our minds not to sin again. Strengthen our wills so that we may do penance, reject temptation, and keep from sin in the future. Fill us with such a deep love for you that we desire to please you in all our actions and words. Then our hearts will not be stony but will be like yours. We will be at peace and look forward to living forever in your kingdom. Amen.*

3. **First reading** Ezekiel 36:25–28 (A Heart of Flesh)

4. **Gospel reading** The Lost Sheep, The Prodigal Son, The Sinful Woman, or Zacchaeus

5. **Examination of conscience** (geared to the age level of the students)

6. **Psalm 51:1–12**

7. **An Act of Contrition**

8. **Procession** Students deposit their stones in the pail.

9. **Song** (Suggestions: "Though the Mountains May Fall," "There's a Wideness in God's Mercy")

10. THE ROSARY (for page 41, 62)

APOSTLES' CREED

■ OUR FATHER

▫ HAIL MARY

☐ GLORY BE

START

Long ago when many people were illiterate, they couldn't pray the daily Church prayer, which included the 150 psalms from the Book of Psalms in the Bible. So instead, they prayed 150 Our Fathers (called Paternosters in Latin), keeping track of the prayers on strings of beads. In the twelfth century, people began praying 150 Hail Marys instead. As they prayed, people meditated on events in the lives of Jesus and Mary, called mysteries, one mystery for each decade or set of ten beads. There were three sets of mysteries: Joyful, Sorrowful, and Glorious. In 2002, Pope John Paul II gave us a fourth set called the Luminous Mysteries or Mysteries of Light, which close the gap between the Joyful and Sorrowful Mysteries by covering the public life of Jesus.

HOW TO PRAY THE ROSARY

Make the Sign of the Cross with the crucifix and pray the Apostles' Creed. On the single bead pray an Our Father. On the three beads pray Hail Marys and pray a Glory Be at the end. Then for each decade, pray an Our Father on the single bead, pray ten Hail Marys, and end with a Glory Be.

OPTIONAL CONCLUDING PRAYER

Hail, Holy Queen, Mother of Mercy! Our Life, our sweetness, and our hope! To you do we cry, poor banished children of Eve; to you do we send up our sighs, mourning and weeping in this valley of tears. Turn, then, most gracious advocate, your eyes of mercy toward us; and after this our exile, show unto us the blessed fruit of your womb, Jesus. O clement, O loving, O sweet Virgin Mary. Pray for us, O holy Mother of God, that we may be made worthy of the promises of Christ.

O God, whose only-begotten Son, our Lord Jesus Christ, has by his life, death, and resurrection purchased for us the rewards of eternal life, grant that through meditating on these mysteries of the Most Holy Rosary of the Blessed Virgin Mary, we may imitate what they contain and obtain what they promise.

THE JOYFUL MYSTERIES

1. The Annunciation The angel Gabriel was sent by God to announce to Mary that God had chosen her to be the Mother of Jesus the Savior (Luke 1:26–28).

2. The Visitation Mary traveled to help her older relative Elizabeth who was pregnant with John the Baptist. When Elizabeth heard Mary's greeting, she cried out, "Blessed are you among women, and blessed is the fruit of your womb." Mary responded with the Magnificat prayer (Luke 1:39–45).

3. The Birth of Jesus Mary gave birth to Jesus, wrapped him in swaddling clothes, and laid him in a manger. Angels appeared to shepherds and sang, "Glory to God in the highest heaven, and on earth peace among those whom he favors" (Luke 2:1–20).

4. The Presentation in the Temple Mary and Joseph presented baby Jesus to God in the Temple as the law required. There, Simeon and Anna recognized that Jesus was the Savior (Luke 2:22–38).

5. Finding of the Child Jesus in the Temple As a twelve-year-old, Jesus remained in Jerusalem after Passover. On the way home his parents discovered he was missing. Three days later they found him in the Temple listening to teachers and asking them questions (Luke 2:41–50).

THE LUMINOUS MYSTERIES

1. The Baptism in the Jordan River Jesus asked John the Baptist to baptize him. John saw the heavens open and the Spirit of God descend on Jesus. A voice came from the heavens saying,

"This is my Son, the Beloved, with whom I am well pleased" (Matthew 3:17).

2. The Wedding at Cana When wine ran out at a wedding, Mary appealed to Jesus and he worked his first miracle. He turned water into excellent wine (John 2:1–12).

3. The Proclamation of the Kingdom of God Jesus proclaimed the good news of God's love and salvation, saying: "The time is fulfilled, and the kingdom of God has come near; repent, and believe in the good news" (Mark 1:15).

4. The Transfiguration Jesus took Peter, James, and John up a mountain. While he prayed, his face changed and his clothing became dazzling white. He spoke with Moses and Elijah (Luke 9:8–36).

5. The Institution of the Eucharist On the night before he was crucified, Jesus shared a meal with his disciples and gave them the Eucharist. He offered himself for us under forms of bread and wine. In the Eucharist he is with us in a special way (Mark 14:22–25).

THE SORROWFUL MYSTERIES

1. The Agony in the Garden After the Last Supper, Jesus went to a garden with Peter, James, and John. He prayed, "My Father, if it is possible, let this cup pass from me; yet, not what I want but what you want." He found the apostles sleeping (Matthew 26:36–46).

2. The Scourging at the Pillar Pontius Pilate, to satisfy the crowd, had Jesus scourged by the soldiers and then handed him over to be crucified (Mark 15:16–20).

3. The Crowning with Thorns Soldiers stripped Jesus and threw a scarlet cloak on him. They made a crown out of thorns and placed it on his head. They put a reed in his hand like a scepter. Kneeling before him, they mocked, "Hail, King of the Jews!" (Matthew 27:27–31).

4. The Carrying of the Cross Jesus, weak from being whipped and beaten, could not carry his cross all the way to Calvary. Simon of Cyrene was forced to help him (Mark 15:21–22).

5. The Crucifixion at Golgotha (Place of the Skull) Jesus was crucified between two criminals. He prayed, "Father, forgive them; for they do not know what they are doing" (Luke 23:33–46).

THE GLORIOUS MYSTERIES

1. The Resurrection Early Sunday morning an angel appeared to two women at Jesus' tomb and said, "Do not be afraid; I know that you are looking for Jesus who was crucified. He is not here; for he has been raised, as he said." The angel sent the women to tell the disciples (Matthew 28:1–10).

2. The Ascension of Our Lord Jesus led his disciples to Bethany. He blessed them, then went apart from them and was taken up to heaven (Luke 24:50–53).

3. The Descent of the Holy Spirit When the disciples were gathered together on Pentecost, the Holy Spirit that Jesus had promised, came to the Church with signs of fire and wind. The apostles courageously went out and proclaimed the good news, and people of every language understood them (Acts 2:1–13).

4. The Assumption of Our Lady into Heaven At the end of her earthly life, Mary was taken up body and soul into heavenly glory.

5. The Coronation of the Blessed Virgin Mary Mary, the holy Mother of God, reigns in heaven as Queen of All Saints. There she prays for and cares for the members of the Body of Christ.

Activities for the Luminous Mysteriers

Here are sample activities to accompany the Luminous Mysteries, used perhaps in the context of a living rosary.

1. *The Baptism of Jesus.* Seventh graders can read a radio interview with John the Baptist.
2. *The Wedding at Cana.* First and second graders can sing the related song from *Stories and Songs of Jesus* (OCP Publications).
3. *Jesus Proclaims the Kingdom.* Third graders can do a cheer with cards labeled "Good" and "N," "E," "W," "S" (for the four directions of the world) as a response to a litany prayed by all from the program.

   Cheer: "Spread the Good News, North, South, West, East!" (Five cheerleaders raise and lower "Good News" cards and then hold card *N* up, card *S* down, card *E* right, and card *W* left.)

   Litany: God created the world and us…
   God loves us as his children…
   After Adam and Eve sinned, God gave us
   a second chance to live with him in heaven…
   God sent Jesus to save us…
   Jesus saved us by his death and resurrection…
   God forgives our sins…
   God's kingdom of peace and justice is coming…

   At the end the cheerleaders shout, "Yea, God!"
4. *Transfiguration.* Sixth graders can perform a skit.
5. *Institution of the Eucharist.* The pastor or another adult can tell the story of the Last Supper and talk briefly about the Eucharist.

11. SCHOOL RETREATS (for page 42)

Throughout the year, each grade level can have a turn making a retreat. Create a progressive display on a school wall or bulletin board by having each group add something after its retreat. Here is a sample program.

JOURNEYING WITH JESUS

Progressive display: A picture of Jesus and a symbol of heaven. The students add footsteps with Christlike qualities written on them; each grade level's can be a different color.

8:30 Mass

9:00 Icebreaker. Give each student a letter of the alphabet and ask each to name something beginning with that letter that he or she would take on a journey.

9:15 to 10:15 Our Life as a Journey

Talk At birth you began on a journey of life. Where are you going? (To our Father in heaven.) Jesus made this journey too. He was born in Bethlehem, lived thirty plus years, and then returned to his Father.

Sometimes your journey is thrilling. You meet different people, see different places, and have wonderful experiences. But sometimes the journey is difficult. Your path is rocky and uphill when you meet up with problems and sadness in life. Sometimes you make detours when unexpected things happen or when you forget where you're going. Sometimes you run and even dance along the way. Other times you drag your feet. Sometimes you may stumble and fall.

At certain times your journey is marked by milestones or special events. What are some of these for you?

Activity (*pass out paper and markers*) On this paper you will make a chart of your life. In one corner draw a cradle with a baby in it. In the opposite corner diagonally, draw a cloud with rays to stand for heaven. Now make a winding path covering the paper that goes from the cradle to the clouds. In the first part of the path write or draw pictures of the main events in your life so far. This can include things like a new friend you made, your family's move to a new house, a hobby you took up, a vacation trip, or your First Communion. As you do this, thank God for the gift of your life.

Now imagine other things that will happen to you along the road of your life and draw or label them on the rest of your path. This time as you work, ask Jesus to be with you throughout your life.

Break

10:30 to 11:30 Jesus Walks with Us

Talk We are blessed. All along our journey of life, we have a companion. Jesus is with us. He lives within and is closer to us that we are to ourselves. We can talk with him at any time. When things get hard, Jesus says to us, "Take up your cross and follow me." When we are tired, Jesus says, "Come to me all you who labor and are burdened, and I will give you rest." Jesus is also with us in a special way in the Eucharist. We call it bread for the journey. In the Eucharist Jesus gives us the strength to keep on the path to the Father.

Jesus called you to walk with him along his way. He said, "I am the Way." The first Christians called themselves followers of the Way. The way of Jesus is the way of love. Jesus wants you to love others just as he did. If we live like Jesus, we will reach our goal of heaven safely. What are some gospel stories that show what Jesus is like? What virtues does he have?

Scripture reading God has given us a map for our journey. It's called the Bible. In it we find directions for how to reach our destination successfully. Jesus gives us a lot of advice: "Forgive each other. Do not store up treasures on earth. Don't judge people. Serve one another. Pray to your Father in heaven." What else does Jesus tell us to do?

William Penn once said, "I expect to pass through life but once. If therefore, there be any kindness I can show, or any good thing I can do to any human being, let me do it now, and not defer or neglect it, as I shall not pass this way again." Jesus was constantly doing things for others. Now let's read about a journey Jesus made to help someone.

Read Luke 8:41–56, the Daughter of Jairus
As you walk with Jesus this year, how would you like to be more like him? Would you like to be more gentle, kind, patient, helpful, truthful, friendly, loving, sharing, courageous, humble, prayerful? Choose one way that you will try to follow Jesus. This can be a virtue or a very specific thing, such as helping your mother or doing your homework without being told.

Footprint activity Give each student a footprint and a sheet of writing paper. Direct the group to write on their footprints one way they will try to follow in Jesus' footsteps. (They shouldn't write their name on the footprints.) Then have the students write a letter to Jesus telling him about their goal and asking for his help. As the students work, play a song about following Jesus, such as "Companions on the Journey" or "Step by Step." Collect the footprints to post on the school bulletin board. Have the students keep their letters and encourage them to put them in a place at home they will see and read them often.

11:30 Prayer
Tell the students that long ago people would journey to holy places such as the shrines of the saints. This was called making a pilgrimage, and the people on the journey were pilgrims. Explain that because we are all on the journey to heaven, we are all pilgrims on earth. During the prayer service, the students may come to the table and pick up a seashell as a reminder of this retreat.

Song A journey hymn such as "Lead Me, Guide Me," "We Will Walk," "I Want to Walk as a Child of the Light," "We Are Marching," "Path of Life," "Sometimes by Step"

Prayer A Vocation Prayer by Thomas Merton (see page 141)

Scripture Word Pass around envelopes with Scripture verses for the students to take (see page 125)

Quiet Time Reflection on the Scripture verse

Story: Footprints One night a man had a dream. He was walking along the beach with the Lord. Across the sky flashed scenes from his life. In each scene he noticed two sets of footprints in the sand: one belonged to him, and the other to the Lord. When the last scene of his life flashed before him, he looked back at the footprints in the sand. He noticed that many times along the path of his life there was only one set of footprints. He also noticed that it happened at the very lowest and saddest times in his life. This really bothered him, and he questioned the Lord about it, "Lord you said that once I decided to follow you, you would walk with me all the way. But I have noticed that during the most troublesome times in my life, there was only one set of footprints. I don't understand why when I needed you most, you would leave me." The Lord replied, "My precious, precious child, I love you, and I would never leave you. During the times of trial and suffering, when you saw only one set of footprints, it was then that I carried you" (Author unknown).

Quiet Time Reflection on the students' hopes for their journey.

Litany The response is "Jesus, walk with me."

> *When I am in awe at the beauty in your world...*
> *When I am happy and glad to be alive...*
> *When I try to do something that is hard for me...*
> *When I fail at something and feel bad...*
> *When I am hurt by other people...*
> *When I have a problem and don't know where to turn...*
> *When I am worried and afraid...*
> *When I am tempted to stray from your way...*
> *When I fail to love and commit a sin...*
> *When I have a chance to show love in a difficult way...*
> Amen.

Procession to choose a seashell from the table.

12:00 to 12:30 Lunch

12:30 A journey activity such as the following:
- A journey of service by going in groups to visit homebound parishioners or a nursing home.
- A pilgrimage to a nearby church or shrine.
- If it is Lent, the stations of the cross.

After the activity, the students can talk about what they did.

Dismissal

12. A HOLY TRIDUUM RETREAT
(for page 43, 63)

Because schools are in session on Holy Thursday, some schools make it a day of recollection. Students carry out activities related to Holy Thursday, Good Friday, and Holy Saturday. The activities may all be held in the same classroom, or the students may travel from room to room, and a different person can conduct an activity in each room.

Suggested activities:

- Make a cross out of wood and wire. Kits are available.
- Decorate a cross as a mosaic.
- Sing songs about Triduum events.
- Put on playlets about the Triduum events.
- Listen to a reading of the passion and reflect on it.
- View a video or part of a video on Jesus' last hours.
- Pray the stations of the cross or watch an enactment prepared by students.
- Color a picture of the Triduum events. These can be found on the Internet and in books.
- Listen to a book or a parable about the crucifixion, such as *The Tale of Three Trees*, *The Giving Tree*, and "The Bamboo Tree."

114 • **Prayer First!**

13. LABYRINTH (for page 46)

Here is a labyrinth that can be enlarged for student use.

14. FAMILY PRAYER HANDOUT (for page 47)

Parents must be acknowledged as the first and foremost educators of their children. Their role as educators is so decisive that scarcely anything can compensate for their failure in it. For it devolves on parents to create a family atmosphere so animated with love and reverence for God and others that a well-rounded personal and social development will be fostered among the children....Let parents then clearly recognize how vital a truly Christian family is for the life and development of God's own people.

■ *Declaration on Christian Education*, #3

25 WAYS TO FOSTER FAITH IN THE HOME

1. Give blessings to one another.
2. Celebrate namedays and baptismal anniversaries.
3. Pray spontaneously at special times: first driver's license, first allowance, first date, tenth birthday, first day of school, or a new job.
4. Pray grace before and after meals.
5. Celebrate the Eucharist as a family. Discuss the readings before Mass and the homily after. Sometimes participate in a weekday Mass together.
6. Set up a prayer corner in your home with religious images, a Bible, candles, and floral arrangements.
7. Pray the rosary together, at least a decade a day, and a whole one each day in May, Mary's month, and October, the month of the rosary.
8. Attend a parish mission, retreat, or prayer service together.

9. Play Christian songs in the car and at home and sing along with them.
10. Visit shrines and other churches.
11. Talk about prayer: the way you like to pray best, your favorite prayer, and when you pray.
12. Pray for situations in the news or your neighborhood and for friends, relatives, and acquaintances who need help.
13. Use religious images in the house to stay mindful of God and your faith: a crucifix on bedroom walls; pictures and statues of Jesus, Mary, and the saints; religious prayers and sayings.
14. Observe religious feasts in your home: set up a shrine for Mary in May, display blessed palm, prepare green food for St. Patrick's Day.
15. Decide what to do as a family during Advent and Lent to observe the season, such as setting up an Advent wreath in your living room and participating in Holy Week services together.
16. Choose a patron saint for your family.
17. Have a blessed family candle and display it on your dining room table for special occasions.
18. Be creative in forming a habit of praying at certain times such as while driving to school or cleaning the house.
19. Memorize Scripture passages or short prayers together.
20. Set aside a certain day each week for family prayer. Take turns leading it.
21. Begin building family prayer traditions, such as reading the nativity story together on Christmas Eve.
22. Pray a novena or triduum as preparation for a special feast or event such as a First Communion or a wedding.

23. Pray a prayer together on special occasions like Father's Day, Thanksgiving, and birthdays.
24. Celebrate the sacrament of reconciliation together.
25. Write a family prayer or a family creed.

POPE JOHN PAUL II'S PRAYER FOR FAMILIES

Lord God, from you every family in heaven and on earth takes its name. Father, you are love and life. Through your Son, Jesus Christ, born of woman and through the Holy Spirit, fountain of Divine Charity, grant that each family on earth may become for each successive generation a true shrine of life and love.

Grant that your grace may guide the thoughts and actions of husbands and wives for the good of their families and of all the families in the world. Grant that the young may find in the family solid support for their human dignity and for their growth in truth and love. Grant that love, strengthened by the grace of the sacrament of marriage, may prove mightier than all the weaknesses and trials though which our families sometimes pass.

Through the intercession of the Holy Family of Nazareth, grant that the Church may fruitfully carry out her worldwide mission in the family and through the family, through Christ our Lord, who is the Way, the Truth and the Life forever and ever. Amen.

15. BACK-TO-SCHOOL PRAYER RALLY
(for page 48)

- Welcome to all: students, teachers, parents, staff
- School prayer and school song
- Introduction of new school personnel, the new class, new students
- Presentation of the new year's motto and goals (option: Begin with a power point presentation or slide show of last year's events)
- Prayer service:

Leader As a Catholic school, we are a community of Christians who follow Christ. We are bound together by our faith in him and our love for him. With the help of his Spirit, our Teacher and Counselor, we will all grow together this year in wisdom, knowledge, and grace. Let us pray for God's blessings on this new scholastic year.

Prayer

*Come, Holy Spirit, fill the hearts of your faithful
and enkindle in them the fire of your love.
Send forth your Spirit and they will be created
and you shall renew the face of the earth.*

*O God, who instructed the hearts of the faithful
by the light of the Holy Spirit,
grant us by the same Holy Spirit
a love and relish of what is right and just
and a constant enjoyment of his comfort,
through Christ our Lord. Amen.*

Scripture Reading Luke 2:41–52 The Finding in the Temple

Intercessions One by one, individuals process up and place a representative object on a table before an image of Jesus, such as the "Jesus the Teacher" icon or a picture of the school patron.

Leader Let us join with the students as they pray to the Lord, our Master Teacher, that their lessons may form them into the best people they can be.

Response Lord, hear our prayer.

Cross or Bible: May our religion classes deepen our faith in Jesus and make us more committed to his Church, his people, let us pray to the Lord.

Writing tablet and pen: May our English classes prepare us to speak and write the truth in order to make a better world, let us pray to the Lord.

Book: May our reading classes give us the tools to understand our world and find the truth and the good in it, let us pray to the Lord.

Globe: May our geography classes give us an appreciation of people in other countries who have different ways and beliefs, let us pray to the Lord.

History book: May our history classes prepare us to be the leaders of the future, let us pray to the Lord.

Ruler and calculator: May our math classes teach us skills of accuracy, perseverance, and problem solving so that we can live successfully in the world, let us pray to the Lord.

Musical instrument: May our music classes bring us the joy of producing beautiful sounds alone and together that lasts a lifetime, let us pray to the Lord.

Paint set: May our art classes heighten our sensitivity to the beauty around us, let us pray to the Lord.

Closing Prayer
Leader And now let us ask Jesus himself to teach us to be more like him.
  All "Learning Christ" (see page 139)

Blessings
Invite the parents to bless their children by saying "I bless you" and making the Sign of the Cross on their foreheads.

Remind the parents that they are the first and primary teachers of their children, but they share this responsibility with the school. Invite the teachers and school staff to stand. Ask the parents to raise their hands over them and bless them while this blessing is read:

May the Lord bless you as you fulfill your task.
May he give you knowledge, wisdom, and patience as you teach our children.
May he fill you with the joy and satisfaction of knowing that you have touched the lives of many people for the better.
And in the end may Jesus greet you with the words, "Well, done, good and faithful servant. Enter into the kingdom of my Father."

16. O ANTIPHONS (for page 55)

The O Antiphons address the Messiah using Old Testament titles. They are prayed during the days before Christmas in the Church's liturgy and are also sung in the song "O Come, O Come, Emmanuel."

DECEMBER 16
O Shepherd who rules Israel, you who lead Joseph like a sheep, come to guide and comfort us (Our Father, Hail Mary, Glory be).

DECEMBER 17
O Wisdom that comes out of the mouth of the Most High, that reaches from one end to another and orders all things mightily and sweetly, come to teach us the way of prudence! (Our Father, Hail Mary, Glory be).

DECEMBER 18
O Adonai and Ruler of the house of Israel, who did appear to Moses in the burning bush, and gave him the law on Sinai, come to redeem us with an outstretched arm! (Our Father, Hail Mary, Glory be).

DECEMBER 19
O Root of Jesse, which stands as an ensign of the people, at whom the kings shall keep silence, whom the Gentiles shall seek, come to deliver us, do not tarry (Our Father, Hail Mary, Glory be).

DECEMBER 20
O Key of David, and Scepter of the house of Israel, that opens and no one shuts, and shuts and no one opens, come to liberate the prisoner from the prison, and them that sit in darkness, and in the shadow of death (Our Father, Hail Mary, Glory be).

DECEMBER 21
O Dayspring, Brightness of the everlasting light, Son of Justice, come to give light to them that sit in darkness and in the shadow of death! (Our Father, Hail Mary, Glory be).

DECEMBER 22
O King of the Gentiles, and desire thereof! O Cornerstone, that makes of two one, come to save us, whom you have made out of the dust of the earth! (Our Father, Hail Mary, Glory be).

DECEMBER 23
O Emmanuel, our King and our Lawgiver, Longing of the Gentiles, and their salvation, come to save us, O Lord our God! (Our Father, Hail Mary, Glory be).

DECEMBER 24
O You who sit upon the cherubim, God of hosts, come, show your face, and we shall be saved (Our Father, Hail Mary, Glory be).

17. STATIONS OF THE CROSS
(for pages 42, 55, 63)

When praying the stations, usually one person carries the processional cross and two carry lighted candles on either side. The three process from station to station. The song "At the Cross Her Station Keeping" is the traditional song used during the stations.

First Station Jesus Is Condemned to Death
Second Station Jesus Carries His Cross
Third Station Jesus Falls the First Time
Fourth Station Jesus Meets His Mother
Fifth Station Simon of Cyrene Helps Jesus Carry His Cross
Sixth Station Veronica Wipes the Face of Jesus
Seventh Station Jesus Falls the Second Time
Eighth Station Jesus Consoles the Women of Jerusalem
Ninth Station Jesus Falls the Third Time
Tenth Station Jesus Is Stripped of His Garments
Eleventh Station Jesus Is Nailed to the Cross
Twelfth Station Jesus Dies on the Cross
Thirteenth Station Jesus Is Taken Down from the Cross
Fourteenth Station Jesus Is Laid in the Tomb

18. NOVENA EXAMPLE (for page 63)

EXALTATION OF THE HOLY CROSS NOVENA

The following prayer is prayed nine days in a row.

Jesus, who because of your burning love for us willed to be crucified and to shed your Most Precious Blood for the redemption and salvation of our souls, look down upon us and grant the petition we ask for (mention here).

We trust completely in your mercy. Cleanse us from sin by your grace, sanctify our work, give us and all those who are dear to us our daily bread, lighten the burden of our sufferings, bless our families, and grant to the nations, so sorely afflicted, your peace, which is the only true peace, so that by obeying your commandments we may come at last to the glory of Heaven.

19. LITANY EXAMPLE (for page 57, 63)

LITANY OF THE HOLY SPIRIT

Lord, have mercy on us.

Christ, have mercy on us.

Lord, have mercy on us.

Father all powerful, have mercy on us.

Jesus, Eternal Son of the Father,

Redeemer of the world, save us.

Spirit of the Father and the Son, boundless life of both, sanctify us.

Holy Trinity, hear us.

Holy Spirit, who proceeds from the Father and the Son, enter our hearts.

Holy Spirit, who is equal to the Father and the Son, enter our hearts.

Response: Have mercy on us.
Promise of God the Father,
Ray of heavenly light,
Author of all good,
Source of heavenly water,
Consuming fire,
Ardent charity,
Spiritual unction,
Spirit of love and truth,
Spirit of wisdom and understanding,
Spirit of counsel and fortitude,
Spirit of knowledge and piety,
Spirit of fear of the Lord,
Spirit of grace and prayer,
Spirit of peace and meekness,
Spirit of modesty and innocence,
Holy Spirit, the comforter,
Holy Spirit, the sanctifier,
Holy Spirit, who governs the Church,
Gift of God, the most high,
Spirit who fills the universe,
Spirit of the adoption of the children of God,

Holy Spirit, inspire us with the horror of sin.
Holy Spirit, come and renew the fire of the earth.
Holy Spirit, engrave your law in our hearts.
Holy Spirit, inflame us with the flame of your love.

Holy Spirit, open to us the treasures of your graces.

Holy Spirit, enlighten us with your heavenly inspirations.

Holy Spirit, lead us in the way of salvation.

Holy Spirit, grant us the only necessary knowledge.

Holy Spirit, inspire in us the practice of good.

Holy Spirit, grant us the merits of all virtues.

Holy Spirit, make us persevere in justice.

Holy Spirit, be our everlasting reward.

Lamb of God, who takes away the sins of the world, pour down into our souls the gifts of the Holy Spirit.

Lamb of God, who takes away the sins of the world, grant us the spirit of wisdom and piety.

Come, Holy Spirit! Fill the hearts of your faithful and enkindle in them the fire of your love.

Let us pray. *Grant, O merciful Father that your divine Spirit enlighten, inflame, and purify us, that he may penetrate us with his heavenly dew and make us faithful in good works; through Our Lord Jesus Christ, your Son, who with you in the unity of the same Spirit, lives and reigns forever and ever. Amen.*

20. SCRIPTURE VERSES (for page 70)

Here are some verses that can be distributed to students.

> Your light must shine before others, that they may see your good deeds and give glory to your Father in heaven. ■ Matthew 5:16

> Whenever you pray, go to your room and shut the door, and pray to your Father who is in secret.
> ■ Matthew 6:6

Do not store up for yourselves treasures on earth, where moth and rust consume, and where thieves break in and steal. But store up for yourselves treasures in heaven. ■ Matthew 6:19–20

Do not judge, so that you may not be judged.
■ Matthew 7:1

Ask and it will be given you; search, and you will find; knock, and the door will be opened for you.
■ Matthew 7:7

In everything do to others as you would have them do to you. ■ Matthew 7:12

Come to me, all you who are weary and are carrying heavy burdens, and I will give you rest.
■ Matthew 11:28

If you have faith the size of a mustard seed, you will say to this mountain, "Move from here to there," and it will move; and nothing will be impossible for you. ■ Matthew 17:20

Whoever wishes to be great among you must be your servant. ■ Matthew 20:26

Do not fear, only believe. ■ Mark 5:36

If any want to become my followers, let them deny themselves, take up their cross, and follow me.
■ Mark 8:34

Be merciful, just as your Father is merciful.
■ Luke 6:36

I am the resurrection and the life. Those who believe

in me, even if they die, will live. ■ John 11:25–26

This is my commandment, that you love one another as I have loved you. ■ John 15:12

Blessed are those who have not seen and yet have come to believe. ■ John 20:29

The Lord is my shepherd, I shall not want.
■ Psalm 23:1

Those who seek the Lord lack no good thing.
■ Psalm 34:10

Faithful friends are a sturdy shelter. Whoever finds one has found a treasure. ■ Sirach 6:14

Do not fear, for I have redeemed you; I have called you by name, you are mine. ■ Isaiah 43:1

When you pass through the waters, I will be with you; and through the rivers, they shall not overwhelm you. When you walk through fire you shall not be burned. ■ Isaiah 43:2

All things work together for good for those who love God. ■ Romans 8:28

Be steadfast, immovable, always excelling in the work of the Lord, because you know that in the Lord your labor is not in vain.
■ 1 Corinthians 15:58

God loves a cheerful giver. ■ 2 Corinthians 9:7

Be kind to one another, tenderhearted, forgiving one another as God in Christ has forgiven you.
■ Ephesians 4:32

21. A "HEART ROOM" PRAYER (for page 73)

Pass out safety pins to the children.

Concentration: Inhale and exhale slowly three times. Hold your safety pin in your hand and look at it. You've probably used a safety pin sometime to keep something together. Maybe when a button has come off, you've used a safety pin to keep your shirt together or to keep your pants or skirt from falling off. Open your safety pin. (If children are very young, open it and show it to them.) Touch the sharp point. The point helps the pin go into things, but it can also be dangerous. Being stuck by a pin can really hurt. Straight pins are pins too, but they are not safety pins. Their points are not protected. At one end, the safety pin has a home for the point to keep it from hurting. Also straight pins can easily slide out of things, but the home on the safety pin locks the pin safely in place so it keeps doing its job.

Meditation: Close your eyes now and think about how our tongue is like a sharp pin. What we say with our tongue can be good and repair bad situations. For example, when someone is sick and we say, "I hope you feel better," that makes the sick person happy. Sometimes though our tongue can hurt people. We can say things that make them sad. Our words wound their hearts. Maybe we call another child names. Maybe we sass our parents. Maybe we tell a lie. When we use our tongue the wrong way, we feel bad. We wish we could take back the words. Our mouths are like the safety pin's home. Sometimes it is better to keep our mouths shut tight and not say the words that first come into our mind.

Contemplation: Keep your eyes closed and go into your "heart room" where Jesus is waiting for you. He hugs you and tells you he's glad to see you. He says, "I know you are thinking about how your tongue can do good and evil. I used my tongue to tell people about God and how much he loves them. I also used it to speak words that healed people's bodies and hearts. I said to deaf ears, 'Be open' and to sinners, 'You are forgiven.'"

Then Jesus looks into your eyes and says, "I want you to say kind words that will help people too. I also want you to avoid saying hurtful words. Whenever you think of a cutting remark that will hurt someone's feelings, do not say it." Jesus goes on. He says, "I know this isn't easy. Sometimes people say mean things to you, and you want to say mean things right back. Sometimes your mom or dad tells you to do something and you're in a bad mood and want to complain or even yell. At these times, do not say anything."

Then Jesus smiles and says to you, "I can help you. Just ask me. That reminds me," he says, "one of the best ways to use your tongue is to pray. Praise and thank God for all the good things you enjoy. And thank God for your gift of speech."

Ask Jesus now to help you control your tongue so that you keep it from hurting others. Then stay with him a little longer, telling him that you love him.

Closing: It's time now to leave your "heart room." Open your eyes. You might make up your mind that from now on you will think twice before you open your mouth and say something that will do damage. You will only say things that will really help people.

22. GUIDED MEDITATION (for page 75)

ZACCHAEUS SEES JESUS

Invite the students to relax. Tell them they may close their eyes if they wish.

Read the story of Zacchaeus in Luke 19:1–10.
Retell the story, putting the students into it and filling in the details.

You are in a crowd of people walking along with Jesus and the apostles. The sun is hot on your head, and the road is rocky and dusty under your feet. Everyone is excited and talking loudly. You notice Zacchaeus, the chief tax collector, in the crowd. People hate him because he works for Rome, the country that is oppressing them. Besides, Zacchaeus has become very rich because he has charged more than normal and kept the extra for himself. Now Zacchaeus is trying to see Jesus, but he is short, so he is jumping up and down in order to see over people's shoulders. Suddenly Zacchaeus runs ahead of the crowd and goes to a sycamore tree. He grabs the lowest branch and hoists his short, plump body up into the tree. He climbs a little higher and is half hidden among the leaves. When Jesus gets to that spot, he stops. You and the crowd all stop too.

You see Jesus peer into the tree and hear him tell Zacchaeus to come down quickly because he wants to stay at his house today. The crowd around you gasps. Zacchaeus scrambles down the tree, his face all smiles. He points the way to his house, and the two begin walking. The crowd starts making angry noises. They complain that Jesus is going to a sinner's house. Zacchaeus and Jesus stop, and you hear Zacchaeus say that he will give half of his possessions to the poor and repay those he has stolen from four times as much. This is twice as much as the law requires. You see Jesus smile. He turns to the people and declares that salvation has come to Zacchaeus's house. Jesus states that he has come to seek out and save the lost.

Lead the students into reflecting on the story.

Just as Jesus seeks out Zacchaeus in the tree, he seeks us out. Jesus wants us to set things right in our lives so that we will be happy. But Zacchaeus might never have been cured if he hadn't been looking for Jesus. We too need to look for Jesus. We need to take time in our lives to be with Jesus, to gaze upon his face, and to read about him in the gospels. Once we've found him, we will know that he loves us and wants to be our friend. Then we can't help being like Zacchaeus and desiring to be the best person we can be. We want to be worthy of Jesus' friendship. Then we will follow Jesus with a light heart. This might surprise everyone, even ourselves.

Invite the students to pray.

Take a few minutes now to talk to Jesus. Tell him you want to see him.... What bad habits in your life do you know you need to change? What steps will you take to change them?... Ask Jesus to forgive you for them and to give you the grace to change.

23. INTRODUCTION TO CENTERING PRAYER (for page 78)

Background: Father Jim and the officers of St. Mary's youth club are meeting at the lake to plan the year's activities. After a day of brainstorming and swimming in the lake, the group sits on the beach talking.

Characters: *Father Jim, Amy, Gina, Mike, Paul*

Mike This has been a great day! I feel really close to God here.

Amy Me, too.

Gina Father Jim, what's your favorite kind of prayer?

Father Well, Gina, I'd have to say centering prayer.

Paul Centering prayer? What's that? Is there a St. Centering?

Father No, Paul. Centering prayer is an ancient form of prayer that is now popular again. It takes its name from the fact that in doing it, you center all your thoughts and feelings on God who lives in the center of your being.

Mike How do you do that?

Father Do you really want to know?

All Sure. Yes.

Father OK. The first step is to quiet down, close your eyes, and think of God within you. You empty your mind of all other thoughts, feelings, and pictures.

Mike That ought to be easy for Gina. Her mind's pretty empty already.

Gina Quiet, Mike. I want to hear this.

Father As I was saying, you think of God, believe in him, and love him. You ask God to let you experience his presence, love, and care.

Paul How long does this take?

Father Just about a minute. Once you're in God's presence, you just rest there, responding to his love with love. You use a prayer word or phrase to keep your mind on Jesus.

Amy What's a prayer word?

Father It's a word or phrase that expresses your feelings for God, like "I love you."

Gina Well, when my sister talks in her sleep, she just says her boyfriend's name over and over. I think I'll say "Jesus" as my prayer word.

Father Wonderful. You repeat this word in your mind while you enjoy God's presence. Whenever other things come into your mind, you repeat the word and it brings your thoughts back to God. It's like a tug on a kite string.

Gina Don't you think about anything else during this prayer—like a gospel story or a problem you have?

Father No, you just give God loving attention and let him surround you with the ocean of his infinite love. It's something like the swimming you did in the lake today.

Gina That sounds beautiful.

Father It is. It's so beautiful that you should end this prayer gradually, perhaps by praying the Our Father slowly.

Paul Otherwise it's like suddenly having the light turned on when you've been in the dark.

Father You've got it.

Amy I don't know if I can do this prayer. It sounds like pretty deep stuff.

Father It's really simple, Amy. Just give yourself over to God and remain in his presence. It's like a little child sitting on her father's lap. The father is so happy to be close to his child that it makes no difference if the child says nothing or even falls asleep.

Amy I see. The important thing is that you're spending time with your friend.

Paul Giving yourself to God.

Father Exactly.

Mike Why don't we plan a day of recollection for the club and teach everyone centering prayer?

Father Good idea, Mike. But don't you think you'd better try it yourself first?

Gina What's stopping us from doing it now?

Father Nothing. Let's pray.

24. TREASURY OF PRAYERS (for pages 15, 39)

DAY BY DAY

Thank you, Lord Jesus Christ,
For all the benefits and blessings you have given me,
For all the pains and insults you have borne for me.
Merciful Friend, Brother and Redeemer,
May I know you more clearly,
Love you more dearly,
And follow you more nearly,
Day by day.

■ St. Richard of Chichester

PRAYER FOR PEACE

Lord, make me an instrument of your peace.
Where there is hatred, let me sow love;
Where there is injury, pardon;
Where there is doubt, faith;
Where there is despair, hope;
Where there is darkness, light;
Where there is sadness, joy.

Divine Master, grant that I may not so much seek to be consoled, as to console; to be understood, as to understand; to be loved, as to love; for it is in giving that we receive, it is in pardoning that we are pardoned, it is in dying that we are born to eternal life.

■ attributed to St. Francis of Assisi

PRAYER OF ST. AUGUSTINE

Breathe in me, O Holy Spirit,
that my thoughts may all be holy.
Act in me, O Holy Spirit,
that my work, too, may be holy.
Draw my heart, O Holy Spirit,
that I love only what is holy.
Strengthen me, O Holy Spirit,
to defend all that is holy.
Guard me, then, O Holy Spirit,
that I always may be holy. Amen.

PRAYER BEFORE THE CRUCIFIX

Behold, O kind and most sweet Jesus, before your face I humbly kneel, and with the most fervent desire of soul, I pray and beseech you to impress upon my heart lively sentiments of faith, hope and charity, true contrition for my sins and a firm purpose of amendment. With deep affection and grief of soul, I ponder within myself, mentally contemplating your five wounds, having before my eyes the words which David the Prophet spoke concerning you: "They have pierced my hands and my feet, they have numbered all my bones."

ANIMA CHRISTI

Soul of Christ, make me holy.
Body of Christ, save me.
Blood of Christ, fill me with love.
Water from Christ's side, wash me.
Passion of Christ, strengthen me.
Good Jesus, hear me.
Within your wounds, hide me.
Never let me be parted from you.
From the evil enemy, protect me.
At the hour of my death, call me.
And tell me to come to you
that with your saints I may praise you
through all eternity. Amen.

MEMORARE

Remember, O most loving Virgin Mary, that never was it known that anyone who fled to your protection, implored your help, or sought your intercession was left unaided. Inspired with this confidence, we turn to you, O Virgins of virgins, our Mother. To you we come, before you we stand, sinful and sorrowful. O Mother of the Word Incarnate, do not despise our petitions, but in your mercy hear us and answer us. Amen.

PRAYER FOR GENEROSITY

Lord, teach me to be generous.
Teach me to serve you as you deserve;
to give and not to count the cost;
to fight and not to heed the wounds;
to toil and not to seek for rest;
to labor and not to ask for reward,
except to know that I am doing your will.

■ St. Ignatius of Loyola

PRAYER OF ABANDONMENT

My Father, I abandon myself to you. Do with me as you will.
Whatever you may do with me, I thank you.
I am prepared for anything; I accept everything.
Provided your will is fulfilled in me and in all creatures
I ask for nothing more, my God.
I place my soul in your hands.
I give it to you, my God,
with all the love of my heart
because I love you.
and for me it is a necessity of love,
this gift of myself,
this placing of myself in your hands
without reserve
in boundless confidence
because you are my Father.

■ Charles de Foucauld

RADIATING CHRIST

Stay with me, and then I shall begin to shine as you shine;
so to be a light to others.
The light, O Jesus, will be all from you.
None of it will be mine.
No merit to me,
it will be you who shine through me upon others.
O let me thus praise you, in the way you love best,
by shining on all those around me.
Give light to them as well as to me;
light them with me,
through me.
Teach me to show forth your praise, your truth, your will.
Make me preach you without preaching—
not by words, but by example
and the fullness of the love which my heart has for you.

ST. TERESA'S BOOKMARK

Let nothing disturb you,
Nothing frighten you;
All things are passing,
God never changes!
Patient endurance
Attains all things;
Who God possesses
In nothing is wanting;
Alone God suffices.

SHINE THROUGH ME

Dear Jesus, help me to spread your fragrance everywhere I go.
Flood me with your spirit and life;
penetrate and possess my whole being so completely

that all my life may only be a radiance of yours.
Shine through me and be so in me
that everyone I come in contact with
may feel your presence within me.
Let them look up and see no longer me—
but only you, Jesus.

■ John Henry Cardinal Newman

ST. PATRICK'S BREASTPLATE

Christ be with me, Christ within me,
Christ behind me, Christ before me,
Christ beside me, Christ to win me;
Christ to comfort and restore me;
Christ beneath me, Christ above me,
Christ in quiet, Christ in danger,
Christ in hearts of all that love me,
Christ in mouth of friend and stranger.

LEARNING CHRIST

Teach me, my Lord, to be sweet and gentle in all the events of life,
in disappointments,
in the thoughtlessness of those I trusted,
in the unfaithfulness of those on whom I relied.
Let me put myself aside,
to think of the happiness of others,
to hide my little pains and heartaches,
so that I may be the only one to suffer from them.
Teach me to profit by the suffering that comes across my path.
Let me so use it that it may make me patient, not irritable.
That it may make me broad in my forgiveness,
not narrow, haughty and overbearing.

May no one be less good for having come within my influence.

No one less pure, less true, less kind, less noble for having been a traveler with me in our journey toward Eternal Life.

As I go my rounds from one task to another, let me whisper from time to time, a word of love to you. May my life be lived in the supernatural, full of power for good, and strong in its purpose of sanctity. Amen.

SERENITY PRAYER

God, grant me the courage to change the things I can change,
the serenity to accept those I cannot change,
and the wisdom to know the difference.
But God, grant me the courage not to give up on what I think is right,
even when I think it is hopeless. Amen.

MARY STUART'S PRAYER

Keep me, O God, from all pettiness;
let me be large
in thought, in word, in deed.
Let me be done with fault-finding
and leave off all self-seeking.
May I put away all pretense
and meet others face to face
without self-pity and without prejudice.
May I never be hasty in judgment
and always generous.
Let me take time for all things, and
make me grow calm, serene, and gentle.

Teach me to put into action
my better impulses,
straightforward and unafraid.
Grant that I may realize that
it is the little things of life
that create differences,
that in the big things of life
we are one.
And, O Lord God,
let me not forget to be kind.

VOCATION PRAYER

My Lord God, I have no idea where I am going.
I do not see the road ahead of me.
I cannot know for certain where it will end.
Nor do I really know myself,
and the fact that I think that I am following your will
does not mean that I am actually doing so.

But I believe that the desire to please you does in fact please you.
And I hope I have that desire in all that I am doing.
I hope that I will never do anything apart from that desire.

And I know that if I do this,
you will lead me by the right road though I may know nothing about it.

Therefore will I trust you always
though I may seem to be lost and in the shadow of death.
I will not fear, for you are ever with me,
and you will never leave me to face my perils alone.

■ Thomas Merton

SIOUX INDIAN PRAYER

O Great Spirit
whose voice I hear in the winds,
And whose breath gives life to all the world,
Hear me! I am small and weak,
I need your strength and wisdom.

Let me walk in beauty and make my eyes
ever behold the red and purple sunset!
Make my hands respect the things you have made
and my ears sharp to hear your voice.

Make me wise that I may understand the things you have taught my people.
Let me learn the lessons you have hidden in every leaf and rock.

I seek strength, not to be greater than my brother,
but to fight my greatest enemy, myself.
Make me always ready to come to you
with clean hands and straight eyes.

So when my life fades, as the fading sunset,
my spirit may come to you without shame.

PRAYER TO ST. JOSEPH

O blessed Joseph, faithful guardian of my Redeemer, Jesus Christ, protector of your chaste spouse, the virgin Mother of God, I choose you this day to be my special patron and advocate and I firmly resolve to honor you all the days of my life. Therefore I humbly beseech you to receive me as your client, to instruct me in every doubt, to comfort me in every affliction, to obtain for me and for all the knowledge and love of the Heart of Jesus, and finally to defend and protect me at the hour of my death. Amen.

SPIRITUAL COMMUNION

My Jesus, I believe that you are present in the Most Holy Sacrament. I love you above all things, and I desire to receive you into my soul. Since I cannot at this moment receive you sacramentally, come at least spiritually into my heart. I embrace you as if you were already there and unite myself entirely to you. Never permit me to be separated from you.

PRAYER OF CHILDREN FOR THEIR PARENTS

O Almighty God, you gave us the commandment to honor our father and mother. In your loving kindness hear my prayer for my parents. Give them long lives and keep them well in body and spirit. Bless their labors; keep them always in your care. Bless them generously for their loving care for me. Grant that, through your grace, I may always be their support and comfort and that after our life together on earth, we may experience the joy of together praising you forever. Amen.

LITANY OF THE BLESSED VIRGIN MARY (LITANY OF LORETO)

Lord, have mercy.
Christ, have mercy.
Lord, have mercy.
Christ, hear us.
Christ, graciously hear us.

God, the Father of heaven,
have mercy on us.
God, the Son, Redeemer of the world,
have mercy on us.
God, the Holy Spirit,
have mercy on us.
Holy Trinity, One God,
have mercy on us.

Response: pray for us.
Holy Mary,
Holy Mother of God,
Holy Virgin of virgins,
Mother of Christ,
Mother of divine grace,
Mother most pure,
Mother most chaste,
Mother inviolate,
Mother undefiled,
Mother most amiable,
Mother most admirable,
Mother of good counsel,
Mother of our Creator,
Mother of our Savior,
Mother of the Church,
Virgin most prudent,
Virgin most venerable,
Virgin most renowned,
Virgin most powerful,
Virgin most merciful,
Virgin most faithful,
Mirror of justice,
Seat of wisdom,

Cause of our joy,
Spiritual vessel,
Vessel of honor,
Singular vessel of devotion,
Mystical rose,
Tower of David,
Tower of ivory,
House of gold,
Ark of the covenant,
Gate of heaven,
Morning star,
Health of the sick,
Refuge of sinners,
Comforter of the afflicted,
Help of Christians,
Queen of angels,
Queen of patriarchs,
Queen of prophets,
Queen of apostles,
Queen of martyrs,
Queen of confessors,
Queen of virgins,
Queen of all saints,
Queen conceived without original sin,
Queen assumed into heaven,
Queen of the most holy Rosary,
Queen of families,
Queen of peace.

Lamb of God, who takes away the sins of the world,
Spare us, O Lord,
Lamb of God, who takes away the sins of the world,
Graciously hear us, O Lord.

Lamb of God, who takes away the sins of the world.
Have mercy on us.

V. Pray for us, O holy Mother of God,
R. That we may be made worthy of the promises of Christ.

Grant, we beg you, O Lord God, that we your servants, may enjoy lasting health of mind and body, and by the glorious intercession of the Blessed Mary, ever Virgin, be delivered from present sorrow and enter into the joy of eternal happiness, through Christ our Lord. Amen.

THE DIVINE PRAISES

Blessed be God.
Blessed be his Holy Name.
Blessed be Jesus Christ, true God and true Man.
Blessed be the Name of Jesus.
Blessed be his Most Sacred Heart.
Blessed be Jesus in the Most Holy Sacrament of the Altar.
Blessed be the great Mother of God, Mary most Holy.
Blessed be her Holy and Immaculate Conception.
Blessed be her Glorious Assumption.
Blessed be the Name of Mary, Virgin and Mother.
Blessed be St. Joseph, her most chaste spouse.
Blessed be God in his Angels and in his Saints.

Appendix 2

CATHOLIC PRAYER WORDS

Adoration the response of praise people give to God as they stand in awe of God's great power and majesty.

Benediction a Eucharistic devotion in which the Blessed Sacrament is placed in a monstrance with which the people are blessed. The priest raises the monstrance and with it makes the Sign of the Cross over all present.

Blessed Sacrament the name given to the consecrated host preserved in the tabernacle, through which Jesus is fully present.

Blessing a prayer calling on God to bestow gifts on a person. A blessing can also ask God to "mark" a certain object or place with favor and divine protection, such as in a house blessing. A blessing can also mark places or objects as grace-giving, for example shrines and rosaries. It can mean the act of God bestowing grace and favors, for instance, we say that God blesses us. On the other hand, we can also bless God, which means to praise God. The United States Bishops publishes a book called *Catholic Household Blessings and Prayers*, which offers many blessings that can be done in the home.

Canticle a sung prayer. There are several canticles in the Bible, most notably the Canticle of Zechariah, Mary's Magnificat, and the Canticle of Simeon, which are all found in the Gospel of Luke.

Centering Prayer silent prayer that focuses on God dwelling in a person's heart. When attention is drawn away from God, a word or phrase is used to come back to God. In essence, centering prayer is simply resting in God, enjoying God's presence. See chapter 11 for a longer explanation.

Communal Prayer prayed together in a group. Jesus promised that where two or three are gathered in his name, he is in their midst.

Contemplation the highest form of prayer, a prayer without words, through which one is totally rapt in God's presence.

Contrition prayers through which people express sorrow for sin, ask for forgiveness, and express their intention to avoid sin in the future.

Divine Office see *Prayer of Christians*.

Eucharistic Devotions special prayers in honor of the Blessed Sacrament, such as visits to the Blessed Sacrament and the rite of Benediction.

Examination of Conscience entails reviewing one's life to discover where he or she has cooperated with God's grace and where he or she has not. It is part of the preparation for the sacrament of reconciliation. It's recommended that an examination of conscience be made each night.

Grace before/after Meals before meals a person or group asks God to bless them and the food they are about to eat. In grace after meals they thank God for their food.

Holy Hour an hour spent in prayer, usually before the Blessed Sacrament. It has its origin in the Agony in the Garden when the apostles fell asleep instead of praying as Jesus had asked them to. When Jesus found them sleeping, he asked: "Could you not watch one hour with me?" People especially make holy hours when the Blessed Sacrament is exposed.

Intention some cause for which a person offers intercessory prayer, such as world peace.

Intercessions prayers that ask for something on behalf of others, for example, the general intercessions prayed at Mass.

Jesus Prayer dating back to the fifth century and especially popular in the Eastern Christian churches, this is a simple intercession: "Lord Jesus, Son of God, have mercy on me, a sinner." It becomes a mantra (see below) when repeated over and over and synchronized with breathing.

Journaling writing one's thoughts and prayers, sometimes daily. This practice makes people more reflective and can lead to a richer prayer life.

Labyrinth a circular path that leads to the center of a circle. As people walk the labyrinth, they pray as they make their way to the center, which stands for God, and then they pray as they make their way back out into the world again. Labyrinths became popular in the Middle Ages when not everyone could make a pilgrimage to the Holy Land. Many European cathedrals had labyrinths in their floors. Today labyrinths are created in lawns and on enormous canvases. They can also be "walked" with your finger on paper. There are also metal and cloth labyrinths, as well as some on the Internet that can be walked with a computer mouse!

Lectio Divina or sacred reading is a method of prayer that originated in monasteries. Its goal is union with God in contemplation. The four steps, which can be done in any order and repeated, are 1) read a Scripture passage and stop when a word or phrase catches your attention, 2) reflect on your word or phrase 3) respond to God in prayer, 4) rest in the presence of God. *Lectio divina* has been compared to Jacob's ladder in the Old Testament that reached up to heaven. See page 66 for a longer explanation.

Litany a long prayer invoking God, Mary, or a saint under many titles. Each group of invocations is followed by the same response, such as "have mercy on us," or "pray for us." Some of the most popular litanies are the Litany of the Blessed Virgin Mary, the Litany of the Sacred Heart, the Litany of the Holy Spirit, the Litany of the Precious Blood, and the Litany of Saints. See page 123 for the Litany of the Holy Spirit and page 143 for the Litany of the Blessed Virgin Mary.

Mantra a prayer word or phrase that is repeated continually as a way to stay in touch with God. Examples are: God have mercy; Jesus, I love you; and the Jesus Prayer (above).

May Crowning a Marian devotion in which a statue of Mary is crowned. This occurs during May because it is her month and on May 31 we celebrate the feast of the visitation of Mary.

Meditation is mental prayer in which people ponder God and the mysteries of their faith in order to better understand them and prayerfully reflect on them.

Mental Prayer occurs quietly in a person's mind as opposed to vocal prayer which is said out loud.

Novena a process of praying for nine days. The practice stems from the nine days that Mary and the disciples prayed while waiting for the Holy Spirit to come at Pentecost.

O Antiphons short prayers that address Christ using Old Testament titles. They are prayed in the liturgy during the days before Christmas and are in the verses of "O Come, O Come, Emmanuel." See page 120.

Octave eight days of prayer. The church observes a special Christmas octave (after Christmas). There is also a Church Unity Octave from January 18th to the 25th, when we pray that all Christian traditions may be one.

Petition asking God for something such as healing, a safe journey, or forgiveness. Jesus encouraged this kind of prayer when he said, "Ask and it will be given you; search, and you will find; knock, and the door will be opened for you" (Luke 11:9).

Pilgrimage a journey to a holy place, such as the Holy Land or a shrine, for religious purposes.

Prayer Service the celebration of a religious theme, which incorporates Scripture, prayers, quiet time for reflection, and hymns.

Procession walking in honor of God usually within a liturgical or devotional service. For example, there are several processions within the Mass, and on Good Friday some people process outside with a statue of Christ.

Prayer of Christians also called the Liturgy of the Hours and the Divine Office, this is the official prayer of the Church in which the entire day is sanctified. Priests and some religious are obliged to pray it, and all Christians are invited to pray it. There are seven times or hours when these prayers are prayed, such as Morning Prayer and Evening Prayer. The prayers are mostly psalms, canticles, and readings from Scripture, along with intercessions. The Prayer of Christians matches the Mass prayers of the season and day.

Psalms 150 prayer-songs in the Book of Psalms in the Bible. They comprise the Jewish prayer book, and now Christians also pray them. All of the psalms are Hebrew poetry. They express different attitudes toward God: praise, lament, contrition, and thanksgiving.

Retreat a period of time when people withdraw from everyday life and activities to focus on God and their relationship with God. A retreat can be a half day or as long as thirty days. Usually a retreat has different prayer activities including time for quiet prayer, talks by a retreat director, and the celebration of the sacraments of Eucharist and reconciliation.

Rosary a Marian prayer in which people meditate on mysteries in the life of Christ while praying Our Fathers, Hail Marys and Glory Bes on a circle of beads. This is an old and well-loved Catholic prayer that originated from the time when ordinary people were not able to read the 150 psalms. In her appearances at Lourdes and Fatima, Mary asked Catholics to pray the rosary for peace in the world.

Stations of the Cross (or way of the cross) is a devotion in which people remember Jesus' passion and journey to Calvary by walking from station to station and praying. Each of the fourteen stations has a cross and art depicting an event of the passion. Some people add the resurrection as a fifteenth station.

Spiritual Bouquet a gift of prayers and good works. It usually lists the numbers of prayers and good works that are being offered for the receiver.

Spontaneous Prayer informal, vocal prayer that is not rehearsed, written down, or prayed by rote using a formula prayer. It is a from-the-heart conversation with God.

Supplication asking God for something for oneself or others.

Taizé Prayer a method of praying that originated with an ecumenical community of monks in Taizé, France. It mainly consists of chanting short prayers over and over, alternating with periods of quiet prayer.

Thanksgiving one of the primary purposes of prayer through which people express their gratitude to God for all his loving acts of creation and redemption. The Eucharist is the ultimate prayer of thanksgiving. The word Eucharist means "thanksgiving."

Triduum three days of prayer and ritual, the best known of which is the Holy Week Triduum of Holy Thursday, Good Friday, and Holy Saturday.

Veneration of a Relic preserved parts of a saint's body, or something a saint has used, or material that has been touched to a saint is displayed in a case called a reliquary and sometimes people honor (venerate) these relics in a ritual of prayer.

Vocal Prayer prayer prayed aloud. It can be either personal or communal.